To Laurie

Best wishes to you in all of your endeavors.

Maria Sutton

The Night Sky

The Night Sky

A Journey From Dachau to Denver and Back

A MEMOIR

Maria Sutton

JOHNSON BOOKS
BOULDER

Published by Johnson Books, a Big Earth Publishing company,
3660 Mitchell Lane, Suite E, Boulder, CO 80301
1-800-258-5830
E-mail: books@bigearthpublishing.com
bigearthpublishing.com

Library of Congress Cataloging-in-Publication Data

Sutton, Maria.
The night sky : a journey from Dachau to Denver and back ;
a memoir / Maria Sutton.
p. cm.
ISBN 978-1-55566-446-6
1. Sutton, Maria—Family. 2. Czeczerska, Julia. 3. World War, 1939–1945—Refugees—Biography.
4. Sutton family. 5. Fathers and daughters. 6. Birth parents. I. Title.
D808.S88 2011
940.54'05—dc23
[B]
2011033508

9 8 7 6 5 4 3 2 1

Printed in the United States of America

This book is dedicated to:

Jozef Kurek, for giving me life;

The people who tried to help me find him;

Every child who has never known a parent;

The millions of displaced persons from all wars
still searching for their lost families;

The friends, relatives, and acquaintances
that encouraged me to write this book;

Wasyl Czeczerski, my mother's beloved brother;

Paul Venckus for bringing me to America;

and

Julia, my mother, the real hero of this story.

“World War II will not be over until all the families have been reunited and accounted for.”

—The American Red Cross

Contents

"Be kind, for everyone you know
is fighting a hard battle."

—Plato

"Write because you owe God the truth."

—Isak Dineson

ONE

The Night Sky

When I was thirteen years old, I overheard a conversation that would change my life. The shocking news would lead me on a worldwide search for a stranger with piercing blue eyes and sun-colored hair, lasting forty-three years.

My quest would take me to the dark green hills and valleys of the ancient Carpathian Mountains in Ukraine, where the woody fragrance of birch trees and new-mown hay fills the fresh, crisp air after a heavy rain. Vicariously, I would see a sunrise over Poland obscured by brightly colored swastikas on warplanes and I would then be taken into suffocating cattle cars, lice-infested *stalags*, and to the Dachau death camp. Further down a country road, I would hear hearty laughter and beer steins clinking with each salute to the Fuhrer's astonishing victories. I would then visit a dark, foreboding, haunted barrack, where disquieting secrets are revealed.

During my odyssey, I would be taken to beautiful castles in Europe, perched atop hills overflowing with pink, yellow, purple, and white flowers, and into the kind hearts of strangers in faraway lands. Gradually, I would learn the family secrets of untold heroism, quiet courage, and a mother's love—and of tragedy, disillusionment, and heartbreak. The truth I'd uncover at the end of my long journey would allow me to give my family the greatest gift, but it would also have the power to destroy me.

The conversation I overheard led me on a worldwide search for three ordinary people who changed the course of my life in ways I could never have imagined:

Jozef Kurek, a handsome Polish officer with blue eyes and blonde hair. Tall, meticulous about his dress, he polished his boots every day. When he smiled, his right cheek dimpled. Everyone he met liked him, including his German captors. He disappeared in post–World War II Germany shortly after my birth. That is the sum of what I knew about Jozef Kurek when I began my quest to find this stranger, forty-three years ago.

Julia Czeczerska—an enigma whose story is as dark and rich as the soil on which she was born. She was no great beauty, nor would she be considered pretty, but she possessed an indefinable, ethereal quality that men found attractive. This special characteristic ultimately saved her life. Her birthplace, Galicia, an area of Eastern Europe, has been ruled by Russia, Austria, Ukraine, and, at the time of Russia's invasion, Poland. Hitler considered her inferior—she was Slavic; Stalin regarded her as a threat. The SS took her from the bedside of her dying mother, into forced labor. The Fuhrer wanted to repopulate conquered territories with only the Aryan race. Julia Czeczerska was my mother.

Wasyl Czeczerski, a fun-loving boy with aspirations of becoming mayor, or governor, even the president of his country. He had a twinkle in his warm, hazel-colored eyes and a mischievous grin. His strength of character and integrity inspired the villagers in Husne and the surrounding region. Everyone in the oblast (province) seemed to know him, and liked him. He had a soft voice, but it didn't detract from his leadership capabilities. Outgoing, spirited, curious about the world, he never realized his dream; but a better dream would replace it. His existence was unknown to me until it was almost too late. Wasyl was Julia's brother.

History had swept these three people from their families and homelands and into a destiny no one could have foreseen.

My saga began on a farm, twenty miles west of Denver, Colorado.

Summer 1952: Golden, Colorado

I was four years old, sitting on the stoop of our two-room home nibbling fried chicken on a cool summer evening. My mother Julia talked softly with me. Paul, my father, was asleep inside. Our house could only be described as a two-room shack with a small kitchen and a wood burning stove. One 40-watt bulb hanging low in the center of the kitchen provided light, and a radio sat on top of a handmade wooden shelf. Dad had covered the walls with newspapers to keep out cold drafts, but the wind howled through the exterior walls of old warped boards, the newspaper barely insulated us from the brutal weather. We slept together in one room; a blanket was suspended from the ceiling on a long, thick rope, hanging between the two beds in our one small bedroom, separating my sister Krystyna and me from our mom and dad. We had no plumbing, so we hauled water from a pump for cooking and washing. I loved to push the red lever up and down until the cold, clear water gushed out. Krystyna and I bathed in a metal washtub that had transported our worldly possessions from Germany: a few pots and pans, blankets, a set of clothes. Still, the place was far better than what we had in the camps. Compared to life in the displaced persons camp, where we'd lived in row upon row of small rectangular buildings, having our own place was gratifying and awesome. We were happy and thankful, and believed we were rich. Even our own private outhouse, just a short walk away, thrilled us.

Every morning Krystyna and I awoke to the deep, booming voice of a DJ playing his "bells-a-poppin" jingle. It was our first introduction to English, and Krys and I cheerfully sang along with the DJ's theme song while Mom busied herself making toast over an open flame, quickly passing the bread over the fire until it browned.

That night on the stoop the sky was blue-black. Denver's distant lights did not dim the stars' brilliance. The sweet smell of clover filled the air each time a gentle wind blew in our direction. The night seemed especially quiet; the crickets' chirping was the sole intruding sound. In Germany, we had lived with thousands of other families in overcrowded barracks and had become accustomed to loud, hurried voices, babies screaming, and the sound of scraping chairs being moved across wood planks.

I finished my drumstick and Mom gently took the bone from my small hand. I stared at a star twinkling brightly in the night sky, feeling happy and content, unaware of the extraordinary circumstances that had brought us here.

September 1958: Denver, Colorado

Catholic Charities had moved us from Golden to Wheat Ridge, a suburb of Denver, where we now lived in a spacious two-story frame house on five acres of land. The house didn't have central heating, but a pot-bellied stove in the huge kitchen kept us warm. We had fully assimilated into the American way of life and Mom began studying for the citizenship exam when I was eight. I fell in love with America as I heard her tutor teach her the Bill of Rights, the Constitution, and the Declaration of Independence. I'd listen intently as she recited the three branches of government and the contributions George Washington, Thomas Jefferson, and Abraham Lincoln had made to the greatness of the United States. Mom was so proud. I often thought Americans were brilliant to have created such an extraordinarily free, open, and democratic government.

My favorite phrases my mom recited, "We the People" and "inalienable rights," inspired me, instilling in me a deep love for my adopted country. At the age of eight I decided I would serve America in some meaningful way and eventually I became a highly trained investigator for the federal government, occasionally working with the Federal Bureau of Investigation and Drug Enforcement Administration on cases requiring skilled interviewing techniques and tracing methods.

The day when my mother would become a citizen finally arrived. She bought herself a new outfit at downtown Denver's Goodwill Thrift Store. I can still see it—a chiffon navy blue dress with large white daisies and a scalloped neckline. She had also purchased, for the first time, a new pair of shoes, and a neighbor loaned her a single-stranded pearl necklace. I watched her as she nervously applied lipstick and combed her hair. For this momentous occasion she had also purchased a small bottle of lilac cologne. She gaily dabbed my wrists, smiling at me as I raised my hand to smell the fragrance. She was trembling and her eyes were misty from joy. When the doorbell rang, Father Kolka greeted her with a corsage, smiling proudly as he pinned it on her dress.

The ceremony at the Denver City Park Auditorium opened with the Pledge of Allegiance. I looked up at Mom reciting each word clearly and loudly, standing tall and dignified with her hand over her heart. I was so proud she was my mother.

After an evening of speeches, songs, and congratulations, we leisurely walked with the other families to our cars. It was a balmy but warm autumn night. The auditorium had been hot and stuffy; towards the end of the evening I became fidgety and sleepy, but as I stepped outside the fresh air energized me. A gentle wind whirled the golden maple leaves, and I felt enchanted by the night's events. It was dark by the time the crowd of two hundred people streamed out of the auditorium, but the parking lot was ablaze with lights and

I easily found my way to our car, skipping ahead of my family and Father Kolka.

Mom was giddy as we backed out of the parking space and coasted toward the main entrance. She and Father Kolka were engrossed in a conversation about what it meant to be an American and didn't notice a twelve-year-old boy who had rolled down his window as we drove by. I smiled and waved at him, thinking he wanted to say something nice to me, but when we got closer, I saw the sneer on his face, and he began jeering, "DP's! DP's! Dirty DP's!" I sank in the back seat, humiliated and embarrassed, hoping no one else could see me, a displaced person. My parents were not truly Americans. I hung my head. I never wanted to hear my mother's stories about the old country again, but soon something would happen to change all that.

July 4, 1961: Wheat Ridge, Colorado

Mom spent the morning at the stove, preparing food for the Polish Club picnic. The smell of hard-boiled eggs, potatoes, and fried chicken filled the kitchen. The Independence Day celebration would be held on Genesee Mountain, in the foothills of the Rockies. I was glad the picnic would be held in the mountains instead of a park in Denver. The Rockies are breathtaking. Pine trees grow from massive, solid rock formations, and water cascades from rugged spouting boulders. Purple and yellow wildflowers grow in the valleys where bison can be seen grazing contentedly. In autumn, the aspen leaves shimmer in the sunlight, filling the mountains with brilliant gold colors. During winter, skiers from around the globe visit the Rockies for world-class slaloming in the fresh, powdery snow. The spectacular sunsets seem to set the snow-covered peaks ablaze with the red, orange, and yellow rays spanning over the vast horizon.

We drove up the winding, steep road to Genesee and parked beside the picnic tables. Antoni and Janka Mucha, friends my mother had known in Germany's displaced persons camps, had arrived a few minutes before us and were setting the large table with paper plates, napkins, and more than a dozen dishes of their favorite foods. After eating, the adults sat around talking and the children headed to the playground.

I felt out of place at age thirteen, not one of the younger children and not yet an adult, and decided to hang out in our 1956 Chevy Bel Air, listening to '60s hits on the radio. I pushed the seat back as far as it would go and leaned into the passenger side, my leg stretched out the open window.

I stared dreamily at the blue sky and listened to bits of the Polish conversation between Janka and Mom, talking about the old country and Germany.

Over the sound of Ricky Nelson singing "Travelin Man" I heard Janka Mucha say, hushed, "They don't know?"

I sat straight up, turned down the radio, and caught the name "Jozef Kurek."

Mom looked in my direction, lowered her voice, and quickly said, "Cisza, cisza!"—Polish for "quiet."

My mother didn't know that I still understood some Polish.

I had overheard this name—Jozef Kurek—mentioned between my mom and dad before, in muted voices, the conversations immediately stopping when I entered the room.

My heart started pounding, the car became stifling hot, and I had to get out. I began walking among the alpines and aspens until the mountain breeze calmed me.

When it was time to leave, I helped my mom and dad pack the picnic basket. There was small talk during the ride home, but I could sense

Mom's anxiety as I stared out the window, oblivious to the majestic scenery.

At home, Dad went to work in the garden and Mom began washing dishes, avoiding eye contact. I silently rinsed and towel-dried the dishes, waiting until we had put everything away before asking, "Who is Jozef Kurek?"

"I don't know who you're talking about."

"I heard you and Mrs. Mucha talking." Softly, I said, again, "Mom, who is Jozef Kurek?"

Her tone grew angry and dismissive. "I have no idea," she said, turned her back, and started to walk away from me.

I slowed my breathing, summoned my courage, and positioned myself directly in front of her. "Who is he? You have to tell me!"

I held my breath and waited as my mother's face turned white; the painful expression on it startled me.

She lowered her eyes and quietly gave me the answer. I stared in disbelief when she told me, "Jozef Kurek is your father."

September 1977: Denver, Colorado

As the nurse wheeled me out of the room with my newborn baby Brad, wrapped in a yellow fleece blanket and snuggly held in my arms, my husband Keith smiled at me, then looking down at the wrinkled, ruddy bundle, asked, "What is it?"

"They didn't tell you? So, what's it worth to know if it's a boy or girl?" Keith was trying hard to contain himself so I gave him a teasing grin and said, "It's a boy!"

Keith's entire face lit up as he took a closer look at the black head of hair peeking out from the blanket. Our son Brad was alert and looked straight into the eyes of his father. It flashed through my mind that my son would know his father—when I had never known mine.

Yet Jozef Kurek's blood clearly ran through my newborn son—he was twenty-two inches long—much longer than the average newborn at birth; no one in Keith's family was tall. I knew somehow that my son would be Jozef's image and I knew he would be tall like Jozef, another of my father's legacies to my children and me.

During the first few months of my son's life, whenever I was awakened from sleep by his cries, as I sat feeding him in the darkness I studied the night sky, thinking about my father being somewhere in the world, under the same star-strewn sky. I envisioned my son already grown, standing taller than Jozef and looking in the same blue eyes, asking him, "Why did you abandon your family?"

If I ever found my father and couldn't bring myself to ask him that question, maybe my son would, and Jozef would have the guts to tell him the truth.

By the time of my son's birth, it had been sixteen years since I'd learned that Jozef Kurek was my father, and I hadn't made any progress in finding him or getting any information about him. After the first revelation, my mother made it clear through the years that Jozef was a forbidden subject.

"Paul is your father, and don't ever think about Jozef again because he is gone and will never come back."

Whenever anyone commented that I didn't resemble my parents, I thought about Jozef. Paul and Julia were medium built and short, with dark hair, while I was tall, thin, and had light-colored hair. I never told any of my friends that Paul was not my biological father; it seemed like a family secret I had to keep. Another reason was that I feared my friends would ask me questions for which I had no answers.

I had always accepted Paul as my father. A kind, quiet man, he worked hard to give us a good life. But there was something deep within my soul that compelled me to search for Jozef. I wouldn't learn what that was until I was forced to confront one of the most painful truths in my life. The birth of my son Brad increased my desire to find Jozef—someday Brad might ask me about his maternal ancestors, and I had no family history to give him.

Keith could give our son the history of his paternal ancestors, going back to the 1800s. He would tell him that his great-great grandmother Emery came to America during the famine in Wales and had died in childbirth and was buried at sea. Brad would learn of Benjamin Sutton, killed by a cannonball during a battle in Missouri, fighting to preserve the Union. He was twenty years old when he died, leaving a young wife and son. Brad would inherit the leather-bound, gold-embossed album that contained his paternal great-great grandfather Emery's original Certificate of Honorable Discharge from the Union Army during the Civil War. Although yellowed with age, America's ferocious eagle is still prominently imprinted on the heavy paper at the top of the legal size document, signed by his regimental commander. I wanted to be able to tell my son that my ancestors had also fought and died for freedom.

By the mid-1990s, my collection of gold-embossed leather albums had grown to twenty-two volumes full of pictures and historic documents for the Sutton family. When Keith's parents passed away, I had acquired a large, tattered cardboard box full of photos. He and his sisters had gone to Iowa to prepare the small, wood-framed house for sale and found the box in the corner of the attic. The family spent several hours sorting through the pictures, taking hundreds of them for their own collections. When they finished, one of his sisters suggested the remaining photos be thrown out. Keith seldom throws anything away and said if no one wanted the remaining pictures, he would take them.

The big box remained in our basement for several years until a blizzard hit Denver, dumping three feet of snow and closing the city for a few days. I brought fifteen shoeboxes downstairs, placing them on the kitchen table and began sorting the photos, most of which had not been labeled. Little by little, Keith and I finally identified almost all the family members.

I sat at our large kitchen island, surrounded by stacks of acid-free archival paper, photo corners, and plastic sheet protectors. I looked at the dining room table, covered with shoeboxes full of photos of the Sutton family, and, as I carefully placed each photo in the album it occurred to me that I did not have a single picture of Jozef, or any of my Czeczerski relatives. My son would not know what my relatives looked like.

Mom had one picture of Jozef, a group photo of about thirty people standing in front of the Altenstadt DP camp administrative building. Jozef, the tallest man in the group, stood next to Mom while she held me in her arms; my sister, Krystyna, stood slightly in front of them. Mom had given me that picture, but somehow I had misplaced it, putting it in such a special location that it could never be found again, even when I turned my house upside down looking for it. The photo had been taken at too great a distance to clearly see Jozef's face, but I had noted his domineering presence—he stood above the crowd, meticulously dressed, muscular. The sunlight had captured the highlights in his thick, coarse, blonde hair.

Over the next several decades I made it an ongoing mission to search all over the world, looking deeply at the faces of tall, blond, blue-eyed men, hoping to find my father. I'd scan movie credits and telephone books for any name that sounded like Jozef Kurek. In my early twenties, I sent letters to German archives, only to learn that no records of my father could be found. I didn't make any progress until the invention of the Internet, but the most valuable information came from conversations with people.

October 1999: Germany

I looked out the window as we descended below the clouds and saw my first glimpse of Germany—the last place Mom had seen Jozef. I thought of my young mother's 1942 trip to Germany in a dusty, hot, cattle car, a foul stench permeating what little air she had to breathe, a stark contrast to my trip in an air-conditioned Boeing 747, with smiling flight attendants serving drinks and meals. I felt queasiness in my stomach, wondering how terrified my mother must have been upon her arrival.

Or did she refuse to consider the potential horror? What was it about my mother's personality that allowed her to survive and maintain her inspiring ability to hope, love, and laugh?

As we flew closer to Frankfurt, I saw fewer houses with red tile roofs, more high-rises, and then the landscape gave way to a large open field. When the jet touched down, I took a deep breath, not knowing what to expect.

After passing through Passport Control and Customs, I heard the harsh, guttural sounds of the German language and in a strange way felt comforted; the cadence of it reminded me of my mom and dad's conversations.

Butch and Mary, our friends for over forty years, had invited Keith and me to visit Mary's relatives with them in Germany. As we sped down the autobahn, we passed a sign for the turnoff to Heidelberg and I thought of Shirley Temple in *Heidi,* my favorite childhood movie. I loved hearing the bells chiming as the goats, bleating excitedly, climbed up the steep Alps to the cottage where Heidi's grandfather lived. He reminded me of Santa Claus with his white beard. He wore leather lederhosen, traditional Bavarian clothing. Everyone tries to convince Heidi her grandfather is cruel, keeping her away from him, but Heidi perseveres and eventually reunites with him; the entire audience is moved to tears at the final scene. The story touched me—Heidi never gave up her pursuit to reconnect with her grandfather. Passing Heidelberg, I wondered if I would connect with my father and have my own happy ending. I felt a bond forming with this country that had such an enormous impact on my life. Being in Europe excited me—it felt like a visit to my homeland.

Our friends Eckhart and Angelica gave us the grand tour: Bavaria, Austria, Lichtenstein, Italy, and then Switzerland. After a day of riding the Swiss cable cars to the highest peak in Samnaun, we sat down to dinner in our chalet, a large, two-story A-frame that had a balcony spanning the entire length of the upper level, a small restaurant, and a cozy lounge area. I felt light-headed from the thin air and high altitude. The Rocky Mountains have many peaks over fourteen thousand feet, but the fifteen thousand–foot elevations of the Alps had left me dizzy.

The landlord wanted to show his gratitude, delighted to have guests during the off-season in the ski resort. Eckhart said if we didn't drink we would insult the innkeeper. I took a sip with each round, forcing a smile as the liquor burned its way down my throat. I felt the table sinking, the chairs whirling slowly as the bartender served us more shots of schnapps.

We finished eating and moved to the lounge that had a large fireplace in the center of the room. The sound of the crackling fire and smell of burning wood reminded me of the pot-bellied stove in my childhood home in Colorado. Toward the evening's end, Eckhart asked me if I wanted to see anything special when we returned to Germany.

Perhaps the combination of the altitude and schnapps gave me the permission to blurt, "Well, it would be very nice if I could meet my father. He might live there."

All I knew was that Jozef Kurek had disappeared in Germany shortly after my birth, after the war.

Eckhart looked at me intently. "If you want to find your father, look to the places your mother has been."

The simplicity of his advice amazed me. My quest had been going off in ten different directions, when all along the truth was that Mom was the direct route to finding Jozef. I laughed silently, thinking about my lifetime of trying to coax the information from my mother, who refused to bring her thoughts back to certain times and places. I would need all the skills I had learned during my time as a federal investigator to pry the information out of her.

The only information Mom gave me about Jozef during her initial revelation in 1961 was that he was a Polish officer and I looked just like him. Whenever I tried to question her for more details, she gave me a stern look and walked away.

When I first learned that Jozef Kurek was my father, I was thirteen years old and didn't know that archives existed in foreign countries. At that age, I could only hope and imagine that Jozef knew where I was. I dreamed that he would find me and visit me someday.

November 1999: Denver, Colorado

I could hear the coffeemaker sputtering and the smell of brewing coffee filled the air as I opened the front door and entered the living room of my mother's small bungalow-style house in Denver, which she and Dad had purchased after Catholic Charities forced them to move from their home in Wheat Ridge because they needed the land for expansion. Sunlight streamed through the two small windows located symmetrically on each side of the fireplace, capturing the red, yellow, and green colors of the flower pattern in the cut glass. Her solid brick house, built in 1908, had a small kitchen with a freestanding white refrigerator and stove. The light oak rectangular table with white inlaid ceramic tiles dominated the room. I poured myself a cup of coffee and sat at Mom's kitchen table, sipping it while she explained what she wanted me to do. I listened attentively while she explained her reasons for changing her health insurance. She handed me a form she needed me to fill out. When I came to the space for her Social Security Number, she told me her card was in the metal box.

The small, aqua blue box was on the highest shelf of her bedroom closet, locked and out of reach, barely visible. Mom kept all her legal documents in it. On her bed, I keyed in the combination, and began looking for the small card.

It occurred to me that Mom had always been mysterious about her birthplace, saying she'd been born in "Little Poland," but never giving the name of the town, even when asked. I leafed through the documents and noticed the papers from Germany and her immigration documents with "Poland" listed as her place of birth.

Something else caught my eye: The German documents showed her date of birth as February 19, 1920, but her U.S. immigration papers stated February 19, 1919. At first I dismissed it as a clerical error, but then my investigative training refused to let it go. I realized it was an intentional misstatement of facts. Typographical errors would have transpired as 1918 or 1929, but not 1920.

Why did my mother give German and/or U.S. officials an incorrect date? Was it vanity, protection for her and her family, an attempt to make herself untraceable, or something more sinister? Perplexed, I made a mental note of the discrepancy and later that night placed her date of birth on my list of mysteries to solve.

Years later when I received her birth certificate from Ukraine, it showed neither 1920 nor 1919. Looking at the official seal of Ukraine that certified the accuracy of my mother's birth date, I knew she had deliberately misled government officials, but why?

I also came across a yellowed document folded in half, her marriage certificate to Paul. I scanned down to her birthplace: Nizne Husne.

I memorized the spelling, returned to the kitchen table and calmly finished the health insurance application, not mentioning my discovery.

I didn't want to upset her. When I came home, I wrote Nizne Husne on a large piece of paper and placed it in my box of clues.

When I was a youngster, I used to keep a shoebox hidden in the corner of my closet underneath some clothes so that my mother couldn't find it. It was filled with letters from German archives and scraps of paper that had my handwritten notes from my conversations with my mom, and from discussions I had overheard. I always hand-carried the shoebox with me whenever I moved to a new home, giving it the same status as my other valuables and the coffeemaker, carefully placing it in the back seat of my car instead of the moving van. I hoped that box of clues would solve the mystery of Jozef and my mother Julia.

TWO

Julia's Story

July 2000

It was a hot summer day and Mom and I were sitting on the front porch of her house in Denver, sipping iced tea and talking about the weather. The old floorboards creaked with each back and forth motion of the rocking chair. I sat on the ragged couch that had been moved out of Mom's living room and had become her afternoon naptime place.

The iced tea cooled us from the scorching sun of Denver. I like Colorado. Denver's air is thin and dry, and breathing it gives you a peaceful sensation. Whenever we visit Keith's family in Iowa, the humidity gives me a clammy, smothering feeling.

Mom rocked contentedly in her chair, looking up at the blue, cloudless sky. I glanced at her out of the corner of my eye, hoping she wouldn't notice I was studying her. I wanted to see her through Jozef's eyes. Separating Julia the mother, from Julia the young woman falling in love with a handsome Polish officer, was difficult. Who was she—a beguiling enchantress that had captured the heart of a dashing military commander, or a country bumpkin who had been taken advantage of?

As I continued secretly looking at her, I imagined the wrinkles on her face smoothed, her hair darkened, and I could see a young girl sitting on the front porch of her house in Husne, looking at the blue sky on a warm summer day, sipping iced tea. How do I go about finding out who my mother was before she became my mother?

I didn't want to disturb the serenity of the moment, but too many days, months, and years had gone by and I knew someday whatever information she had would eventually be lost, forever. Eckhard had given me good advice that the direct route to Jozef was through her, yet I wasted many precious years waiting for the right moment to ask her the questions I desperately needed answered. My mind quickly ran through a number of questions that I hoped would reveal her true person—the person Jozef knew her to be. But what was the precise question I could ask her? It had to be connected to the war because that is what brought her to Jozef. Not finding the question I needed, I merely asked, "What do you remember most about the Russians in Husne?"

My question surprised her; a distant look came into her green eyes, and shaking her head slowly, as if refusing to relive that moment, she told me, "The Russians shot our good friend and neighbor. He had five young children and a wife, and didn't want to get on the train to Siberia."

"What did he say that made them want to kill him?" I asked.

"No one heard. The Russian soldier didn't even look angry; all of a sudden he shot my neighbor five times, then shoved his body out of the way and continued loading the train."

Mom hesitated to say more, but after a few moments she said, "I felt like I could die at any time."

We sat in awkward silence; I didn't know what to say. I had studied WWII in high school and knew about the Holocaust, but for some reason thought brutality toward civilians was limited to the Nazis. I contemplated how to bring her back to a more happy time when she was that young girl sitting on the front porch of her house in Husne waiting for her life to begin. I asked her to tell me what it was like in Husne before the invasion. I wanted to return Mom to the serenity of her rocking chair and knew she would be happy to recall this part of her life. She had often cheerfully described her childhood in the lowlands of the ancient Carpathian Mountains. She smiled and began describing her homeland, "Alpine wildflowers covered the hills, and snow covered the mountaintops, even in summer. We had many different trees in the forest: fir, spruce, beech, and oak." She started to giggle. "Wasyl loved to climb the trees. I remember one day a big crow had made a nest in one of the giant oaks and Wasyl wanted to see the fledglings. Just as he got to the top of the tree, a big black crow came swooping down on him, fiercely pecking his head, face, and arms, screeching like a monster. I've never seen anyone scamper down a tree as fast as he did that day!"

We laughed, and then she continued, "The grass grows from the valleys to the top of the mountains. There were stacks of hay scattered throughout the countryside. It rained a lot in Husne, so the air always felt fresh and crisp. I loved the smell of wood and freshly mowed grass after a heavy rain. It's very green in Ukraine."

I thought about how different her childhood home is from Colorado, which is arid and mostly brown. The Rockies, west of Denver, are covered with evergreens, but the plains to the east are dry and brown, except for a few patches of green where farmers irrigate the land.

Czeczerski farmland, Nizne Husne, Ukraine, 2009.

Denver would be a stark contrast to Husne, where emerald green carpets of grass cover every square inch of land.

"We owned cows, an ox, horses, and raised pigs and poultry. Cows grazed throughout the valley. I can still hear them mooing from a distance. We also raised sheep. My mother made clothes and blankets from the wool, using a spinning wheel and weaving block."

I tried envisioning my mother as a farm girl, dutifully milking cows—or was she the daughter of a privileged land owner overseeing the management of the farm, and what did Jozef think of her in this scenario? While Mom continued the narration of her life in Ukraine, my mind wandered between images of Jozef and her as young people whose destinies would soon collide.

"Ukraine has dark, rich soil, and everything grows easily there, but the wild animals came down from the forests at night and devoured the crops. Wasyl and I took turns guarding the garden in the middle of the night. If a bad storm came when it was my turn to scare away the wild animals, Wasyl would trade nights with me." The image of my mother as a hard working, fearless girl began to emerge—the kind of woman Jozef would admire.

"Many villagers worked for us during the harvest. Mihas, my stepfather, dreamed of some day buying an American tractor. He had lived in America for close to ten years when he was a young man. He told us stories about life in the United States, and all the technological advances. Wasyl and I listened excitedly whenever he spoke, dreaming that someday we too would visit America.

"We could see Mount Pikui, [one of Ukraine's prominent peaks at 4,610 feet], from the front door of our house. During the summer Wasyl and I hiked up the mountain to eat the wild raspberries, blueberries, and strawberries growing there—they were so sweet and juicy! I used to ski Mount Pikui. Wasyl and I were the best skiers in the village—no one could keep pace with us when we raced down the mountain." So far so good, I thought. Mom was athletic, like I envisioned Jozef to be, another trait that would have drawn them together.

Mom's face suddenly looked sad, her eyes glistened as she said, "I miss Wasyl. I wonder where he is now, and if he still skis."

I realized at that moment how much my mother loved Wasyl. I decided once I found Jozef, I would begin searching for her brother. Thinking about Wasyl and Mom skiing, my thoughts wandered to the world-class slopes of Colorado's ski resorts, and why Mom had never skied them. Before I could ask her, she stated, "Wasyl and I hid in the mountains during the war. Wasyl risked his life to bring me food."

"He was a good brother to you," I commented, feeling I had not known how much she adored her brother because she rarely talked about her family.

"Yes, we were the best of friends, and we had fun in Husne. We caught trout and catfish with our bare hands in the stream down a short hill from our house. I teased Wasyl unmercifully about being a better fisherman than he." Mom continued her stories of their childhood: galloping their horses into the mountains, secretly smoking cigarettes behind the house, and privately laughing until their sides hurt at some of the happenings in Husne. Mom's stories confirmed that she had a good sense of humor. I envisioned her and Jozef sharing smiles and laughter as they began to fall in love, and it would have been a fiery love because there was no doubt in my mind that Jozef would be passionate about love and life.

"We had a good life." Smiling, Mom said, "Wasyl wanted to become president of Ukraine—and I think he could have."

"What was he like?" I asked.

"He was short, but solidly built, and he had brown hair. He had warm hazel eyes and a round face. Everyone liked and trusted Wasyl; they respected his honesty. He had a subtle strength of character; he could have been a good leader for Ukraine."

"What were your aspirations?"

"I wanted to be a nurse," she responded. This too fit my image of what Jozef would want in a wife: a caring, compassionate woman.

Mother continued, "I had a good future—and I owned land and a house in Husne. When my mother's sister Oluzia became terminally ill, her husband abandoned her. I agreed to take care of my aunt, and when she died, I found out she had named me heir to her estate, which included a house on a large acreage of land. Oluzia's husband was furious." This bit of news presented a complication. Did Jozef and Mom split because she wanted to return to Husne after the war to reclaim her estate but Jozef's allegiance to Poland would not allow him to give up his homeland? Did ownership of property stand in the way of their love? The sound of Mom's voice interrupted my thoughts.

"Wasyl was set for life, too. Some day he would inherit the large acreage of the Czeczerski land, which covered several mountain ranges. We had a good life and were making plans for a bright future."

"Did you ever think you could lose it all?"

"We thought about it all the time. Wasyl and I used to walk throughout the Husne countryside, picking up apples, pears, and hazelnuts, storing them in the shed that he and your grandfather Mihas built from large stones hauled from the Carpathians for 'The Black Day.'"

"What's The Black Day?"

"It is the day our country would be invaded again. Ukraine has been invaded so many times, we knew eventually a Black Day would come."

"Did you suspect that Russia or Germany might invade Ukraine?"

"No, but a strange thing happened a few years before the war. One day, sometime in the mid-1930s, Wasyl and I could see dust being stirred in the distance by a black limousine. The older boys barricaded the road through town with large boulders to get a closer look at the fancy car. A dignified high-ranking government official sat in the front seat, dressed in a black suit and white gloves. He looked at the barricade and got angry. He ordered the local police to remove the large rocks immediately. The police nervously scrambled to obey his orders, glaring at the boys while they moved the heavy stones. Villagers talked about the incident for months. It was the first time Wasyl and I had seen an automobile, and it thrilled us!"

But the official visit was an omen. The Black Day that Wasyl and Mother had feared came sooner than expected—Hitler and Stalin invaded Poland and Ukraine a few years later.

"I remember the day the war started as if it were yesterday. It was late Friday night and Wasyl and I had just finished pitching hay. It was hot and muggy; I had been sweating in the field all day and had dust all over myself. I went into the house to get cleaned up before our friends came over to listen to the radio—we were the only family in Husne that had a radio. It was battery-operated because Husne had no electricity, and we cranked it up every Friday night to listen to the two comediennes broadcasting from Lviv. When I came out of the house several of our friends were excitedly standing around the radio. At first I thought the two comediennes had said something especially funny, but when I looked at the faces in the crowd that had gathered at our house, I knew something was terrifyingly wrong. The sound on the radio crackled, but the frenzied news reports of the attack could be heard through the static and sharp humming of the radio.

"As soon as everyone heard that Germany had attacked Poland, panic spread throughout the village. Farmers gathered pitchforks, rakes, shovels, axes, and knives to defend our homeland, and the police told us to tape our windows to prevent shattering by bombs. Warplanes flew over Husne and villagers ran for cover whenever they heard the engines' drone. We heard that Cossacks attacked Russian tanks on horseback, throwing Molotov cocktails, and then quickly fleeing into the deep forests before the Red Army could react."

"Did any bombs fall on Husne?"

"No. We were a farming and lumber community. Hitler and Stalin were bombing strategic targets—military bases and factories, not farms.

"Wasyl and I both worried when one of the reports notified listeners that all able-bodied men must report to command centers to be conscripted into the Polish military. Wasyl's allegiance was not with Poland. He considered Poland an occupier of his own country. He would have gladly put on a uniform to defend Ukraine. As a teenager, Wasyl fought for Ukraine's independence from Poland. He would never even consider wearing a Polish uniform."

I wondered if this were the reason Mother had rarely talked about her family and hadn't stayed in touch with them. Had they disowned her because she had married a Polish officer? Or had Jozef requested she should no longer contact her family because they were anti-Poland? I should have asked her, but by the time I thought of it, she was already excitedly talking about the invasion, and I soon learned that to know about Jozef and Mother's relationship, I would need to relive WWII. I hadn't wanted to go down this path, but this was the road that would end at Jozef's front door.

"Wasyl and I intently listened with dismay to the news of the invasion of Poland and Western Europe, hoping the violence would not reach Husne. Ukraine, Galicia, and Poland had been invaded many times, and the attack was yet another war we would need to survive.

"Two weeks after Germany invaded, the Russian Red Army, red stars painted on their tanks, crossed the Polish border at night, and attacked the entire eight-hundred-mile eastern border, advancing without opposition. They distributed leaflets, 'We have come to liberate the population from the Polish yoke.' The Polish army, frantically defending the western front, couldn't re-deploy to defend eastern Poland. Stalin's tanks advanced into the towns and villages without any resistance. Wasyl didn't even think of it as an invasion, more like Russian soldiers just walking into Ukraine.

"We stayed close to the radio listening to the feverish news reports of the Russian and German advances. We didn't have any weapons to protect ourselves. When Austria and Poland occupied our country, they confiscated our weapons—guns, bows, arrows, and sometimes even nets and fishing poles. They thought we might rise against them, and sometimes they just liked to show us who was boss."

Mother continued, "When news got worse, villagers throughout Husne began preparing for survival—hiding food and water and digging underground shelters. Wasyl quickly dug a cellar near the Czecz-erski home for the family.

"The Red Army entered the town of Turka on September 17, 1939, and established a Soviet administration there, less than thirty miles from where we lived. Less than a week later, Lviv, the capitol of Galicia, about seventy-five miles east of Husne, surrendered to the Red Army, and Russian soldiers began occupying all of Galicia.

"We were afraid of the Russians. The Soviets deported anyone perceived as hostile—teachers, lawyers, businessmen, policemen, priests, and landowners. Stalin sent more than a million Polish and Ukrainian citizens to Siberia.

"We feared Stalin more than Hitler. Stalin was ruthless—he forced an artificial famine and starvation on the Ukrainians. We tried to live normal lives, but we didn't laugh much anymore, and we could no longer be free to roam the green hills of Husne. When we looked at the beautiful mountains, it was to see if soldiers were advancing," Mom recalled with sadness.

Continuing, she said, "Within a few weeks, Russian soldiers overran Husne, ordering the villagers to comply with their demands. They helped themselves to anything they wanted and families stayed locked up in their homes."

With an angry voice, Mom told me, "Once, Wasyl was in the barn, scooping grain to feed the cattle, when a Russian soldier barged in, demanding to know what he was doing. Another time, I was eating homemade ice cream on a hot summer day and a Russian soldier insisted that I give him some. He ate the ice cream too fast, got a sinus headache, and pulled out his revolver at me! I had to convince him that I had not tried to poison him. I knew that the slightest provocation or misstep could cost me my life."

The Russians raided the countryside to conscript men for the Red Army. Our friends, young men, hid in the Carpathian Mountains. KGB agents staked out their homes, and when they returned for food and to check on their families, they were shot to death on their front doorstep.

"Your grandfather Mihas became terminally ill with stomach cancer in the middle of the war. Wasyl took him to Turka for treatment, but the doctor could only give him pain medication. When they returned to Husne, Mihas moaned in pain for two days, before dying in Wasyl's arms in February of 1941. Wasyl buried him near the bell tower by the church, placing a small wooden cross to mark the site, hoping at war's end he could replace it with the traditional large, elaborately sculptured stainless steel cross on a granite base, bordering the grave with a three-foot wrought iron fence.

"Your grandmother Maria was heartbroken and inconsolable," Mom told me. "She used to be so cheerful, always telling us everything would be okay, but now she looked worried, although she never said so.

"Dead soldiers, horses, and livestock were strewn throughout the village. When typhoid hit Husne in 1942, many children died drinking polluted water. The smell of death and the sound of flies buzzing on animal carcasses filled the air. Wasyl volunteered to serve as a driver during the epidemic, taking people in our family's horse-drawn carriage to the hospital in Turka.

"When we heard that Germany had turned against Russia, we knew it wouldn't make a difference to us, because we would lose our independence no matter which country would win the war."

Mother said, "Husne's Jewish population realized they were in great danger from Hitler; the Nazis began rounding them up for deportation to Germany and the concentration camps. The SS officially notified the villagers that anyone assisting the Jews in escaping would be executed. Wasyl was brave and risked his life to take many Jewish families to the train station in Turka so they could escape to non-occupied countries.

"German soldiers soon began raiding Galicia for healthy men and women to be taken into forced labor. My mother, along with most of the older people in Husne, did not go into hiding, nor did children younger than twelve because they wouldn't be taken into Germany—except for the Jews. Wasyl and I, young and healthy, were perfect candidates for forced labor.

"Wasyl and I hid in the hills of the Carpathian Mountains, under bridges and brushwood, and in our family's cold, dank, dirt cellar. The snakes, mice, and rats came into the cellar. When we finally felt it was safe, we came out of the cellar covered in mud and lice. The safest places were in the Carpathian Mountains, but the wild berries didn't provide sufficient food, and water was scarce."

The entire continent of Europe was embroiled in war. Following its victory in Poland, Germany invaded Denmark, Norway, France, Belgium, Luxembourg, the Netherlands, Greece, Yugoslavia, and Holland. The Nazis had created a highly effective and efficient war machine—the number of days from invasion to surrender ranged from eleven to sixty-two. Shortly after invading Poland, Russia began occupying Finland, Estonia, Latvia, Lithuania, and Romania as a part of their Non-Aggression Pact with Germany, which identified Stalin's and Hitler's spheres of influence.

"Throughout Europe," my mother said, "piercing, deafening gunfire could be heard and the rapid fire of machine guns shattered the quiet of cattle grazing in the valley. We heard explosions in the distance frequently. Wasyl and I looked at each other every time we heard an explosion. We were afraid we'd never see each other again—and we haven't," she said sadly.

"During the Russian occupation, movement was highly restricted, but once the Russians were redeployed to defend Stalingrad and Leningrad, we could move more freely, so I left Husne."

This seemed out of character for Mom. "Why did you leave your family at such a dangerous time?" I asked, thinking that if she could abandon her family at such a perilous time, maybe Jozef had not been the one to abandon us—perhaps it was she who had abandoned him!

"I was tired of hiding in the snake-infested dirt cellar. Once the Russians left, I saw my chance to move to a bigger city and try to have a normal life. I didn't want to leave Wasyl or my mother but I felt compelled to strike out on my own. I understood how fragile life was, and I wanted to fulfill my dream of becoming a nurse while I still could. War was chaotic, but I needed to feel normal and made up my mind that the war wasn't going to keep me from getting what I wanted out of life."

She told Wasyl of her plans to move to Skole, an affluent ski resort about thirty miles northeast of Husne. He understood, not wanting to stand in her way, and told her not to worry, that he would take care of their mother and the other children.

"I moved to Skole during the transition from Russian to German occupation of Galicia. Compared to Husne with its eighty-seven residents, Skole was a big city with a population of over six thousand, and I easily found a job as a health and childcare worker for a wealthy family."

My mother seemed happy to recall her early move toward an independent life. I listened as she rocked back and forth in her porch rocker. I thought about her subsequent capture by the Germans. Mother had often described that terrifying night to me and as the scene played through my mind, I realized I didn't know the details. The precise facts of where and when she was brought to Germany were critical to finding Jozef.

"How did you end up in Germany?" I asked.

She responded, "My mother sent me a letter to say that Wasyl had been captured and that she was very ill and could no longer manage the farm. With Mihas dead and Wasyl in a labor camp, she feared they would starve. Without hesitation, I told my employer in Skole that I must immediately return to Husne. Traveling was severely restricted during the German occupation, and I asked my employer to help with travel arrangements. I don't know how he did it, but my wealthy employer managed to get me safely back to Husne.

"When I walked into the house Mother was asleep and disheveled, her forehead warm. I kneeled and whispered, "Mom, I'm home, don't worry, everything will be okay," but she didn't stir. I stayed by my mother's bed, watching her sleep. My sisters, Kazia, Polusia, and Anna, sat quietly in the kitchen. The house was cold. I looked around for something to eat but could find no food. I went to the storage shed where I found some onions and potatoes, then brought a pot of water from the well to make soup.

"Husne was no longer the vibrant village of my childhood. The houses had become dilapidated and the church was in need of repair. Tall weeds hid the graves in the cemetery and covered the farmland. The village seemed to be deserted, eerily quiet, except for a crow flying by, shrieking."

Mother smiled as she remembered Wasyl as a boy scrambling down the large oak, a big crow pecking fiercely at him. She rocked in her chair and smiled, "I miss Wasyl's laughter and his mischievous grin.

"When the soup was ready, Kazia, Polusia, and Anna ravenously gulped it down. I brought a bowl to Mother's bedside, propping her up on the pillows. Tears streamed down her face. We didn't make conversation. I remembered a vivacious Mother, the person everyone had turned to for strength and encouragement; now, I had to be strong.

"I was twenty-four years old when I returned to Husne. I felt responsible for the family's safety and survival of the war. There was no place to escape, even if I had wanted to."

I told my mother, "It saddens me to think of you living in fear, trying to survive, and not enjoying a young woman's life, going to parties, seeing boys, pursuing your career as a nurse."

My mother looked at me as if to say such notions are frivolous. She simply said, "I never thought of any of that. We had to survive, and that's all we ever thought of."

With battles raging all across Europe, there were fewer German soldiers raiding the small villages for people to be taken into forced labor. Whenever word got out that soldiers had been seen, people hid in the mountains and cellars until they left.

"Mother gave me a picture of the Virgin Mary to take with me to the dirt cellar, for comfort and protection when I was in hiding. Her own mother had given the picture to her for protection during the many invasions of their homeland. Although printed on a very thin, tissue-like paper, the holy picture was in excellent condition.

"During late spring of 1942, Mother became deathly ill and ran a high fever, so I slept in the house that evening, rather than hide in the cellar. In the middle of that cold and rainy night, while everyone slept, German soldiers stormed the house, guns pointed, and demanded everyone to '*Raus! Raus*!' ['Get up! Get up!] I jumped to my feet and stared down the barrels of three automatic rifles pointing at me. I stood motionless—afraid the slightest flinch would trigger a hail of bullets. One of the soldiers grabbed my arm, jerking me away from Mother's bedside, and shoved me toward the door.

"Mother, in a deep and fevered sleep, could not be awakened. An SS soldier jammed his rifle barrel in her back. The soldiers agreed the *schweine* wasn't worth taking; she would soon be dead. Neither did they take Kazia or my other sisters; they were too young. But I was old enough, healthy and strong.

Najświętsza Panno, Królowo Polski,
módl się za nami !

The picture of the Virgin Mary my mother hid from the Gestapo and took with her to the Dachau Death Camp, circa early1900s.

"I pointed to my bare feet; the soldier nodded I could get my shoes. I quickly grabbed the picture of the Virgin Mary my mother had given me, and hid it in my shoe. The soldiers didn't allow me to pack. The SS rushed me from the house still in my long, gray flannel nightgown—it billowed in the wind—and loaded me into a truck, taking me to a train. I was in that filthy cattle car for three days. The train stopped once in Czechoslovakia where the Nazis allowed the Red Cross to give us soup, bread, and coffee. The Red Cross gave me a dress to wear for my trip to Dachau."

My heart sank when I heard her final destination was Dachau. I knew she had survived the death camp, but is that the place she had met Jozef, and, if so, what would be the implication?

"By the time we got to Germany, I was exhausted. When the train screeched to a halt, German soldiers slid the doors of each cattle car open, banging and commanding, '*Aus—aus!*'

"I nearly fell as I stepped from the train onto the ramp. My knees were wobbly, and I had a difficult time walking toward Dachau's elaborate entry gate. The stench from the cattle car had made me nauseous, but as I jumped from the train into the open air, the smell of burning flesh terrified me."

All prisoners arrived in Dachau by train, and then walked to the camp on a large asphalt street called "the turnpike to hell." Many prisoners died on the trains from suffocation, dehydration, disease; some committed suicide. Seeing bodies piled alongside buildings, some prisoners created a disturbance, preferring to be shot to death rather than face the horror within the barbed-wire fences.

"I tried to calm myself as I neared the administration building and stood in line with the other prisoners, but a wave of terror hit me. The SS officer hardly looked up from his desk when he asked my name, date and place of birth, parents' names and religion. He did a quick survey of my appearance, and directed me to another line."

Prisoners not murdered and cremated upon arrival were taken to an area enclosed with high, barbed-wire fences. They slept in unheated barracks on three-tiered bunk beds with no mattresses or bedding.

"I followed the large group of prisoners toward the barracks. We stopped in the building that housed the incinerators. The SS told us that if we caused trouble, we would end up in the ovens. Fearing for our lives, we quietly walked into the barracks, the SS snarling orders at us. I collapsed on my assigned bed."

Mother arrived in Dachau in 1942, when Hitler began his systematic exterminations of the Jewish people. It was a dangerous time, but Mother was a spunky young woman, five feet tall, who had a strong personality and always spoke her mind, even with some SS officers.

As I sat with her on her porch in Denver a lifetime later, my mother told me this story:

"A German officer discovered my picture of the Virgin Mary that I had hidden. I told him that, even if he destroyed the picture, the Virgin Mary would protect me. The officer gave me a stern look before handing it back and asked me if I liked Hitler.

"If I say 'yes' I will be killed for lying," she told him. "If I say 'no' you will kill me for not liking the Fuhrer." The officer laughed.

When Mom told me about this confrontation, I was amazed and

puzzled that she had risked her life by being so bold. I speculated her daring bravado would have excited Jozef. Mother was not a physically beautiful woman. She was short and stocky, and did not possess the striking looks that men find so attractive that they overlook otherwise unacceptable behavior.

"He could have sent you to the gas chamber right then and there, or shot you on the spot!"

Top: Dachau barracks, circa 1940s.
Right: Interior of Dachau barracks, circa 1940s.
Above: Incinerators at Dachau Death Camp, located adjacent to gas chamber.

Mom just laughed. "He wouldn't do that to me."

It occurred to me that Mom has always had a sixth sense about judging people. She could easily read a person's character, and connect with them. Mom instinctively knew what to say or do to relate with a person at a basic level. Throughout my life I have witnessed this special gift of hers and people's acceptance and admiration of her audacious, but non-threatening behavior. It has amazed me many times. Perhaps the SS officer spared her life on a whim because he found her candor and energy refreshing, or on a more practical level, because she was young and healthy enough to be worked to death.

Mother claims that it was my grandmother Maria who saved her from the gas chambers by petitioning Hitler, informing him that her daughter had been born in Breslau, Germany, and was German, not Polish. Grandmother demanded that Hitler return her daughter to her home. This story awed me and I wondered if I would have had the same courage.

When they became prisoners and slaves of the Third Reich, my mother and her brother Wasyl were in their mid-twenties. She ended up going to Bavaria, an eight-hundred-mile journey in a filthy cattle car. Wasyl had traveled nine hundred miles in a suffocating coal car to the Stuttgart area, near the Swiss border. Both Wasyl and Mother corresponded with Maria after their capture, but neither ever saw their mother again. I often wonder how anguished Grandmother Maria must have been at the loss of her two children, and I admire her courage in writing to Hitler, demanding that he return her children to her.

Mother remained in Dachau for one month, until the SS officer informed her of good news. A farmer in Starzhausen needed her to work on his farm. The officer explained to her that she would be working for a family that had a small tract of land and a beer garden.

"I told Antoni that you will be the perfect worker. He needs someone lively and energetic to keep his customers happy, and I said I had just the right person for him," the officer said.

The officer had taken a liking to her. Whenever he stopped by her barrack, he would ask her about the Virgin Mary picture, saying, "I see the Virgin is protecting you." She would flirtatiously respond, "Yes, she is."

I have often speculated if there were more to her relationship with the SS officer. Mother was a young woman in a hostile and cruel environment in Dachau and I contemplated their association. Did she like him, or did she exploit his attraction to her to cull favors from him? What did she have to do to survive? I have never asked my mother about her relationship with the commandant although I am intrigued by it. Mother had shocked me when she told me Jozef was my father; I didn't want to deal with another revelation that didn't fit my image of my mother. If she were intimate with the officer, she kept that part of her life private. But whenever she spoke of him, I saw a sparkle in her eyes. I will never know why he was drawn to her, but can only guess that it was because she was a young woman, not Jewish, and was lively and vibrant under the worst possible circumstances—a breath of fresh air in a horrific death camp.

The next morning, my mother was taken from Dachau to Pfaffenhofen, the forced labor transition center. Antoni Breitner came for her and drove her from Pfaffenhofen to his farm on the back of his motorcycle, thundering down the road at ninety miles per hour. She had never seen a motorcycle before, much less ridden on one. The motorcycle's exhaust backfired periodically, scaring her as Antoni drove the thirty-five miles to his house, leaning the massive bike at forty-five degree angles while maneuvering the curves in the road.

At the Breitner farm, Antoni introduced my mother to his family and showed her around the house, informing her of her duties. They walked down to the cow barn and the musty smell of the damp straw reminded Mom of her home in Husne. She began to relax a little, comforted by the familiarity of her surroundings.

The horse stalls were on the opposite side of the cow barn. As Antoni and my mother walked toward the stalls, she saw a good-looking young man busily brushing down the horses. He had a quiet dignity about him. He stood straight and self-assured, but at the same time relaxed and friendly, which struck her, considering his status as a prisoner. He spoke to her in a friendly voice, "I'm glad you're here. Now, I will have someone to speak Polish with me. I'm sure we'll become good friends." Jozef Kurek's presence immediately calmed her.

"So those were the first words Jozef spoke to you?" I asked rhetorically, feeling happy that my image of him as a friendly, outgoing man had just been confirmed.

"I fell in love with him instantly," Mom said.

"Why?" I asked.

"He looked at me with those crystal clear blue eyes and gave me a warm friendly smile. He was so handsome and dignified—a strong man. He made me feel safe."

As I thought about her comments, I began to wonder what went awry.

October 2003: Munich, Germany

I studied the gigantic map that had been installed on the wall of the subway station. Our friend Mary searched for the line that ended in Dachau, while Keith, Mary's husband Butch, and I surveyed the long passageways of the brightly lit subway. Mary quickly found our destination and we proceeded to one of the many stores in the underground to buy our tickets.

As the train sped towards our destination, Mary nervously told us that Dachau is a forbidden word for many Germans; they don't like to associate "what happened in Dachau" with the German people. She told us that some Germans still believe that the accounts of mass murder and torture are exaggerated; some refuse to believe they occurred at all.

I have a friend who lived in Germany in the mid-1950s. He heard many comments from the German people such as, "If the Americans had left us alone, we could have taken care of the Russians for them." A young German woman proudly proclaimed that as a leader in Hitler's youth program, she had the power of life and death over six hundred girls. Her haughtiness sent shivers down my friend's spine. The woman went on to say that when the war ended, everything she had believed in was destroyed, and the only difference between her and my friend was in the "teachings you received from your parents." Her words made a lifelong impression on him.

Mary didn't tell her relatives she had agreed to take us to Dachau. Her uncle, a kind, generous man who Mary loved, had served in the Hitler Youth Corps. Mary didn't want to stress him by letting him know she was going to tour Dachau.

When we exited the train and climbed the steps back into daylight, I saw several buses and taxis waiting to take tourists to visit the remnants of torture. As we entered the compound, I was struck by how empty it looked. I had expected to see row upon row of barracks, but the large area only contained an administrative building, a museum, the crematorium, and a formidable memorial sculpture of black metal for the victims of the Holocaust.

Keith, Butch, and Mary went on the tour while I stayed behind to visit the administration building for a records check. Dachau was a critical stop in retracing my mother's steps; she had stayed in Dachau prior to being transferred to forced labor and I hoped the records would show her transfer location. Dachau records have been fully computerized and the archivist patiently input the name *Czeczerska,* using a number of variations in the spelling, but could not find her.

Despite Germany's reputation for impeccable record keeping, I knew the Dachau records had to be incomplete because my mother had certainly passed through there. She does not have a tattoo with a prisoner number on her arm to prove it, but the Dachau archivist informed me that only the Auschwitz concentration camp tattooed their prisoners; the other camps used badges for identification. I have not been able to verify this fact. Mother had described Dachau to me in great detail, but the records didn't seem to include prisoners who'd merely stopped in Dachau for transition into forced labor, and I believed that the Dachau archives should have contained the names of all those who passed through its gate.

When I caught up with Mary, she had just exited the museum and was clearly touched by what she had seen.

Mary said, "The German people really had no choice. They had to do what they did, or they and their families would be killed."

I was taken aback by her comment. "I can't understand it," was all I could say.

The tour of Dachau was painful for me as I tried to envision my mother walking through these gates and sleeping in the crowded barracks, with no mattress or blanket to keep her warm. Dachau's museum describes in detail the horrors that occurred here. I had difficulty imagining Mother being held in this haunted place.

I looked up at the sign the Nazis placed at the entrance to the camp, to prevent prisoners from revolting: *Arbeit Macht Frei—Work Will Set You Free.* I was surprised by how small and innocuous it appeared, not the massive, evil-looking icon I had imagined it would be.

While walking the grounds of Dachau, it was hard for me to picture my kind, caring mother spending time in what must have been one of the worst places on earth. She would have been the one to give comfort to the other prisoners. As I scanned the eerie site, I thought of her surrounded by barbed-wire fences, German soldiers holding guns,

and vicious dogs. A chill ran through me and I felt a lump in my throat as I envisioned her bravery when she confronted the SS officer. I looked around the empty grounds. I didn't know it then, but Dachau would be the key to solving the mystery of Jozef's disappearance.

THREE

Jozef's Story

"Jozef and I were political prisoners," Mom said one evening in late spring. I had been watching the evening news with Tom Brokaw, not paying close attention to her description of the afghan she was knitting while she sat in her recliner in front of the TV set in her living room. "What did you say?" I asked.

"He and I were prisoners! Not because we had broken any laws, but because of politics—so we were political prisoners."

The term confused me; I began thinking they had been revolutionaries, insurgents, political activists, or better yet, spies who had been captured and sent to prison. I became intrigued with the possibility that Jozef was a spy, especially when one of my friends, an avid reader of Tom Clancy novels, informed me that the only logical explanation for Jozef not being recorded in any of Germany's or Poland's archives would be that he was a spy, possibly a double agent, and had used many pseudonyms, or the German government was protecting him.

The theory appealed to me because it fit the image of the Jozef I had concocted. I began fantasizing about Jozef being a dashing, daring spy, a 007 Pierce Brosnan with blonde hair. A womanizer who had left my mother because there were so many Bond girls out there ready to seduce him and he couldn't resist the temptation. Did my mother leave him because of his infidelities, or did he leave her because he didn't want to be tied down?

I entertained these fantasies until one day Mom said I could get his records from the International Red Cross in Geneva, Switzerland, stating he had been a prisoner of war—the first time she had ever used that term instead of "political prisoner." When I got home I sent an email to the IRC, requesting Jozef's POW certificate. When I got it, the certificate showed that he had been captured in Deblin in October 1939. Deblin is the location of the Polish School of Eagles, the equivalent of the U. S. Air Force Academy. It was also where the Polish Air Force had been headquartered. The news that Jozef had been captured in Deblin excited me. I concluded he was a cadet in training to become a pilot.

I researched World War II battles and discovered that Jozef's location on the exact day of the invasion was Hitler's first target. I tried to envision what Jozef witnessed during the blitzkrieg.

September 1, 1939: Deblin, Poland

On this Friday morning, Jozef would awake to the shrieking of air-raid sirens and the roar of warplanes. I imagined him having an adrenaline rush as he dressed in his uniform—but not from fear. He would be angry that Germany had dared to invade Poland's air space and would have quickly dressed in his uniform, run to the command center to get his weapons, and then jump into his PZL P.11 fighter aircraft, at the time considered to be the world's most technologically advanced fighter plane; he would be determined to totally destroy the arrogant German *Wehrmacht*. As Jozef looked up at the sky, he would have seen hundreds of warplanes with brightly colored swastikas obscuring the sunrise.

He would also have seen that the airport and runways had been pummeled, and Polish pilots and soldiers frantically regrouping to defend the Deblin Fortress and evacuate the pilots and airplanes. Deblin was Poland's military center and a critical strategic target for Hitler. The airport had already been destroyed and the Deblin Fortress was under heavy fire.

Luftwaffe bombers and fighter planes maintained their ferocious assault on Deblin for a full week. The Polish army abandoned the Fortress on the eighth day. Two days later, on September 11, the Polish soldiers destroyed the remaining stored ammunition and retreated eastward to Warsaw and Poland's western borders to protect their country. When the blitzkrieg was over, the German Panzer tanks entered Deblin, followed by the infantry.

Jozef, along with thousands of other Polish soldiers in Deblin, were lost in the chaos of exploding ammunition and retreat. Heavily armed German soldiers in tanks besieged the streets of Deblin and the Fortress, surrounding the entire area, but somehow my ingenious father managed to escape.

Proud Nazi troops goose-step march for the Fuhrer in Warsaw, September, 1939.

With the capture of tens of thousands of soldiers and the retreat of the remaining army, the Deblin population was left defenseless and rushed to stores to get any available food.

Poland had been unprepared for the attack. Germany's strategic destruction of military targets left it defenseless and on October 6, 1939, German and Soviet forces gained full control of Poland. Hitler celebrated the victory by parading through the heart of Warsaw.

Hitler's Victory Parade through the heart of Warsaw, Poland, September, 1939.

As I researched the invasion, I speculated about what type of man my father was, and looked for clues as to why Jozef may have disappeared from my life.

Jozef was a young man of twenty-three, on the threshold of realizing his dream of being a pilot, when Germany invaded Poland. Strong and fearless, Jozef would have loved his freedom and his country. His father's blood had probably paid for Poland's independence and it must have enraged him that Hitler could think victory would be easy. Jozef would have had an intense hatred for the Nazis and there was probably no doubt in his mind that he would reclaim his homeland. If he had any dark thoughts about a Nazi occupation of Poland, he would have dismissed them as being preposterous. He would have a burning desire to be free and would not have been able to envision a defeated Poland.

As I absorbed the reality of what my father must have lived through, I had to wonder if it occurred to Jozef that all may be lost, or did he maintain a glimmer of hope for himself and his country? Did he think that Poland would once again be taken off the world maps? I began making a list of the questions I would ask my father when I found him.

If I could say anything to Jozef about the invasion, it would be to let him know it was not possible for Poland to have won the war on that day. Hitler had been planning and preparing for the invasion for many years, and had superior resources, both in the training of the German soldiers and manufacture of military weapons and equipment. No country was prepared for World War II—not Poland, Great Britain, France, or the eight other countries Hitler invaded in Europe. I wondered if Jozef would scoff at me. Will he disapprove of my analysis of the war? Will he be angry at me or at the injustice, or will he just quietly agree with me that victory was not possible for Poland.

I envisioned my reunion with Jozef: We would meet at an airport, smile, embrace, and then go to a quiet restaurant for dinner where we would sit in a secluded corner to talk about our lives. I would start the conversation with Germany's invasion of Poland, and I hoped he would be impressed with my knowledge of WWII. Or would he be perturbed that I was being presumptuous, or worse yet, would he think that women shouldn't concern themselves with a man's business? I realized I didn't know anything about my father and decided I would let him take the lead in the conversation and refrain from making comments until I got a better feel for his expectation of me. The only thing I knew for certain about the initial meeting was that I wouldn't ask him the question: Why did you abandon your family? I hoped he would answer it without my asking, and that the answer would be an extraordinarily good reason.

I researched the history and found that the circumstances under which Jozef was captured during the invasion would remain a mystery until I found him. His POW certificate states that he was captured on October 4, 1939, thirty-five days after Germany's initial invasion. I pictured Jozef evading German soldiers in the deep forests of Poland, hearing the constant rapid-fire of machine guns in the distance, wondering how he got captured. Or did he surrender when the Panzers surrounded the Fortress and escape was not possible? Wanting to believe my father took heroic action to evade capture and save lives during the invasion, I dismissed my government experience that told me the lapse of thirty-five days may have been just an administrative procedure of annotating the record on the date the prisoner was identified.

What did my father feel at the moment of capture: fear, anger, humiliation, relief? I tried to envision Jozef surrounded by German soldiers and being escorted at gunpoint with other captured soldiers. As he walked to the holding pen, he would have surveyed the horrific sight of soldiers with missing arms and legs, torsos blown open, mangled bodies of the dead covering the streets, and smelled the horrific stench of burning flesh. Perhaps he had witnessed the grisly death of his closest friend. The blue sky would have been filled with black, billowing smoke from burning buildings and he would have walked among the rubble of a completely destroyed city. Did the experience of that day profoundly change him in such a way that he could easily walk away from his family, or was there another, more troubling reason? I tried thinking about what that extraordinarily good reason for Jozef abandoning us could possibly be.

The Nazis had captured more than 215,000 Polish soldiers, and the Russians would apprehend hundreds of thousands more during their invasion. Captured soldiers were forced to march long distances, often as far as eighty miles to German-constructed holding pens. Despite injuries, exhaustion, and bleeding feet, they had to keep pace or be shot. Transfers from the *dulags,* the transit camps, to *stalags,* the permanent prisons, began in December 1939.

As an officer, Jozef would have been more extensively interrogated than other prisoners because he would have information not known by lower-ranking soldiers. After questioning him, the Nazi's sent Jozef on a three-week, 580-mile trip in an overcrowded dirty train filled with other hungry and debilitated prisoners, en route to Germany. The train stopped several times a day to allow the prisoners to relieve themselves, surrounded by guards, with police dogs barking viciously. The Nazis permitted the Red Cross to distribute food. When the prisoners arrived, jeering, hostile crowds met them. German shepherd dogs growled, nipping at their heels, and German soldiers compelled them along with

Captured soldiers wait to board trains that will take them to Germany's overcrowded stalags, circa 1940s.

the butts of their guns. Jozef would have surveyed the crowd defiantly, not as a defeated, humiliated soldier whose country had just been annihilated.

The Third Reich took Jozef to Stalag VII-A, located about twenty miles northeast of Munich in Moosburg, Germany; it would be his home from 1939 to 1941.

Wanting to know every minuscule detail of Jozef, I spent hundreds of hours in front of my computer researching prisoners of war. Thousands of websites described what it was like to have been a POW during WWII. I reconstructed what Jozef may have experienced during the two years he had been held captive by the Third Reich.

Built for 10,000 prisoners, Stalag VII-A grew overcrowded when more than 100,000 captives became part of the population, as a result of Hitler's astonishing victories. Prisoners didn't have sufficient space to sit, stand, lie down, or move around. They were covered with lice, and the smell of sweat pervaded their clothing. Daily, thousands of prisoners flooded the gates. Guarded by 8,000 German soldiers, the camp had 2,000 medics and 170 military chaplains. Two hundred Poles and 900 Ukrainians were the first prisoners. The prison body would eventually swell to represent 72 nations.

Upon Jozef's arrival, German soldiers sheared his blonde hair, and stripped and deloused him, inoculating him with the same syringe used for every prisoner. By now a hungry and tired Jozef would have stood in line for hours before registering and receiving a prisoner of war tag.

It's hard not to envision a defiant Jozef enduring the long registration process, then I can picture him frustrated and angry, collapsing on a skimpy, straw bed, after finally arriving at his flea-infested barrack, surrounded by barbed-wire fences and guards in watch towers. I never visualized Jozef as being afraid—my image of him was that of a brave, fearless man.

The next morning, Jozef would have awakened to German soldiers barking orders and assigning work duties. Most involved cooking, cleaning, mending clothes, and sewing shoes. Prison officials had established the workshops to repair and sew clothes and shoes because the threadbare and tattered clothing of newly arrived prisoners had become a major problem.

The prisoners were constantly hungry. Food became scarce because the Red Cross trains were being bombed. The prisoners were forced to eat soup made from grass and worms. Occasionally, the Germans dumped a truckload of near-rotting potatoes on the grounds. The POWs would experience diarrhea and vomiting from eating rotten food. The barracks would have a constant stench from the digestive problems. Jozef, a meticulously clean man, would have found the situation abhorrent, but would show compassion toward the suffering of his fellow prisoners. He would analyze how he could get invited to join the German officers attending lavish parties in the town of Moosburg, where they were well fed, eating meat and drinking beer and wine.

Jozef's day began each morning at six with German soldiers banging on the door of every barrack, shouting "*raus, raus*," followed by roll call. He would then be allowed to shave. Breakfast was eaten inside the barracks. Prisoners were permitted to go outdoors, but always under the watchful eye of German soldiers. Occasionally, gunshots could be heard. Prisoners trying to escape were shot immediately, without warning. I speculated that Jozef would have performed his assignments enthusiastically and dutifully, knowing that creating the slightest disturbance could lead to his death, but he also wanted to win the confidence of his captors. His time in captivity was monotonous routine. It would have been difficult for the energetic Jozef to be confined to a small space with nothing meaningful to do. Despite the opportunity my father may have had to read a variety of books, the repetition of cooking, cleaning, and meager meals would have left him miserable, although he would not have shown it. The Nazis permitted most POWs to correspond with their next of kin and, shortly after their arrival in the camp, gave them a preprinted postcard to check off the appropriate box: "I am well, I am not well; I am wounded, I am not wounded." No other information was allowed, and the SS screened all correspondence. Jozef sent his preprinted postcard to his sister Stanislawa, indicating that he was well.

Reichsmarks given to prisoners of war, circa 1940s.

The Nazis gave some prisoners the chance to work outside the camp, paying them in Reichsmarks, but they could only spend the money in authorized shops in nearby towns. Most prisoners purchased only toothpaste and shaving soap.

In general, American prisoners of war received much better treatment than their Polish, Russian, or Jewish counterparts, who were tortured and exterminated. Some American prisoners reported that they received adequate treatment and were even allowed to play sports and watch movies. Polish and Russian prisoners were treated poorly because they were Slavs and considered inferior. Of the 5,700,000 Soviet POWs, over three million died in captivity.

Jozef's survival instincts and zest for life would help him endure life in the *stalag*. Although he hated the Germans, he would have known his life depended on befriending them, and would hide his disdain for the Nazis by stifling his arrogance, portraying himself as a congenial person wanting to make the best out of a bad situation. He had an advantage over the other prisoners because he stood out in a crowd and looked Aryan—tall, muscular, with blonde hair and stern blue eyes, a sharp contrast with the other prisoners. Many a Gestapo officer would have been taken aback by his Nordic appearance, thinking a true Aryan had been falsely imprisoned.

I conjectured Jozef would take advantage of this benefit and quickly learned to speak German. His friendliness would earn him special treatment from his captors. The Germans considered him one of their own, and probably offered him cigarettes, shared amusing stories, and allowed him to roam the prison.

But this would not be enough for Jozef, who longed desperately for something more: his freedom from the Nazis, the camp, and the war. He would see them as obstacles to overcome and would begin analyzing how to manipulate the situation for his gain. The Nazis presented Jozef with a partial solution to his desire to regain his freedom.

As more and more German citizens were joining the war effort, an acute labor shortage threatened Germany's ability to manufacture weapons and food. People from occupied countries were not brought in quickly enough to supply the great need for workers. The Nazis began offering some POWs the chance to work in forced labor, provided they renounced their allegiance to their country's military and became civilians. POWs volunteering for forced labor could either work in factories or farms. Most wanted to work the farms because the food and conditions were significantly better than in the factories, where prisoners often worked eighteen-hour days alongside the sick. Contagious diseases plagued the factory slaves, and the work was dangerous. Prisoners were given small food rations while manufacturing munitions, military equipment, steel helmets, and other items needed for Germany's war effort.

I'm sure Jozef struggled for several months before reaching a decision. He was a survivor and would get what he wanted, no matter the consequences. He finally made up his mind: any price would be worth the cost of his freedom. Since he was well liked in the *stalag,* the SS offered Jozef the coveted assignment of working on a farm.I understand and can forgive his betrayal of Poland. His decision would give me life. Fate sometimes plays an important role in our very existence.

When I first began my research on POWs, I'd given myself the task of finding a picture of a tall prisoner whose face resembled mine. I spent hundreds of hours on the Internet, scrolling through thousands of photos of Polish prisoners, but did not come across anyone who could be Jozef. I also spent many evenings and weekends at the Family History Center of the Church of Latter Day Saints, scrolling through microfilm of all Third Reich prisoners with a surname beginning with "K." I contacted military archives in Warsaw, whose records contained photos of 385,000 Polish soldiers—my hundreds of hours attempting to find a picture of Jozef in a potential inventory of half a million pictures available to the public from many different sources did not produce a single photo of Jozef.

When I Googled "Polish Prisoners of War," I found many websites for the Katyn Massacre. One of the Katyn websites had a list of thousands of Polish officers massacred by the Red Army and buried in a mass grave. I clicked on the letter "K," quickly scrolling down to the "Ku" section. To my astonishment, Jozef Kurek was listed. I hit the back arrow to read about the massacre. I discovered that if the area of Poland where Jozef lived had been invaded by Russia instead of Germany, Jozef might not have survived the war at all.

Stalin had committed one of his most heinous crimes in Katyn Forest, near Smolensk, Russia. During Russia's invasion of Poland, 180,000 Polish soldiers were captured. Of those, 15,000 Polish officers and intellectuals were segregated by the Red Army into different detention centers and transported to the same area used by the Bolsheviks in 1919 for murdering Tsar Nicholas's officers. The 15,000 captured officers and intellectuals were loaded into trucks and told they were going home. But the trucks stopped in Katyn Forest and, one by one, each officer was executed with a bullet to the head and buried in a mass grave.

The Institute of National Memory, an agency of the Polish government, has inscribed Jozef's name on the memorial wall honoring the murdered men. I knew it was not possible for my father to have been a victim—the massacre occurred in 1940, many years before my birth—but this was my strongest lead, to date. I believed that, since his family had not heard from him during the war, they presumed he died at Katyn and had placed his name on the wall. If I couldn't find Jozef by other methods, I decided, I would track down his family through the Katyn Memorial records.

While researching prisoner-of-war reports to understand what Jozef may have experienced so I could understand him in some way, I became absorbed by the treatment of POWs, learning that the earliest recorded history of prisoner torture dates back over two thousand years ago. Treatment of prisoners of war was not officially recognized until The Hague IV Convention in 1907 addressed the Laws and Customs of War, enacting twenty Articles relating to the humane treatment of prisoners. During WWII, Katyn was not an isolated case of mass murder; it also took place in Japan, where, through a combination of rage at seeing their own soldiers die at the hands of the enemy, lack of sufficient food to feed their own, and being unable to manage the disarmament and containment of 10,000 POWs, Lieutenant Colonel Cho ordered the machine-gun killing and burial of them in a mass grave. After WWII, the Geneva Convention of August 12, 1949, expanded the Articles from twenty to 143, yet countries to this day continue to mistreat POWs.

Disturbed by the accounts of POW mistreatment and mass murders, I asked my husband Keith how normal people could treat other human beings with such hatred and venom. Keith had seen combat in Viet Nam, and I hoped he could give me insight into how people's general nature could become altogether lost during war.

Keith's response was, "War can change people."

I contemplated his statement. Scholars continue to study how ordinary citizens can turn into sadistic murderers. Hitler has been one of the most studied leaders in modern history, with behavioral scientists conducting experiments to learn under what conditions normal, well-balanced individuals, husbands and fathers who love their families, can turn into savage killers. My mother claimed to have seen Hitler in a parade. "He was standing in his limousine, waving to the crowd. He looked straight ahead, unsmiling, but his presence electrified the crowd into frenzy! They screamed with excitement and there was mass hysteria at the mere sight of him."

I thought about the scene Mom had described. Hitler had a phenomenal talent to rouse and inspire millions of people, but he used it for evil purposes. If he had exploited his extraordinary leadership skills to bring Germany out of a deep depression by improving the economy, giving the German people a high quality of life and standard of living instead of making war and committing genocide, he would have been remembered as a great leader and not a diabolically evil mass murderer.

I thought about how the choices Hitler made had changed the course of history, and I wondered if the war or the choices Jozef made had changed him. If so, how? Keith's temperament had not been changed by his experience in Viet Nam; he was a kind, thoughtful person who helped anyone in need. I hoped that when I found Jozef, he would be a caring person whose spirit or conscience had not been destroyed by the brutality of war.

As I thought about war atrocities, I realized two murderous dictators controlled the fates of my father Jozef, my mother Julia, and her brother Wasyl, and that I was extremely fortunate that they were not among the millions of people killed by Stalin and Hitler. Having integrated only a microscopic version of the events Jozef had experienced from the invasion and imprisonment, I pondered whether Jozef had looked at the stars of the night sky while in the prison in Moosburg, wondering what the future would hold for Poland, and for him.

FOUR

Julia and Jozef

October 2001

One cool autumn day while Mom and I were in our usual places on the front porch of her house, I asked her about her time in forced labor on the Breitner farm, and if Jozef ever talked about his family, hoping to learn the first name of his mother and father. My mother said Jozef rarely talked about anything except the war and the military. She couldn't remember his parents' names.

I pressed her harder.

Staring at the floor, she finally stammered that she thought Jozef had been named after his father who had been killed during WWI, when Jozef was a young boy, about four years old. Mom said that he had a sister, and that his mother was an excellent cook—no one could make *golabki* and *pierogies* like she could.

Pausing, Mom said that Jozef's mother's name may have been Jadwiga or Victoria, and then continued her recollection of the Breitner family.

On the evening of the day that my mother first met my father, she found him in a small corner of the Breitner kitchen.

Mom told me, in a matter-of-fact way, "Jozef's voice was calm as he spoke of the conditions in the *stalag* he'd left, but it was clear he felt distressed. He told me about the starvation, sickness, monotony, and humiliation that led up to his decision to renounce his allegiance to the

Polish army and become a civilian. That's how Jozef came to work for the Breitner's in Starzhausen."

The Breitner's tract of farmland was located across the street from their large house, where the adjoining beer garden was located. A thick forest lay beyond the acreage. Every Saturday night, farmers came to the beer garden where they raised their beer steins in toast to the Fuhrer. They laughed heartily at how easy it had been for Hitler to conquer Europe. My mother refilled the beer between the clinking of the steins with each round of salutation. At the end of the evening, normally not lasting beyond 10:00 p.m., the farmers sang Germany's national anthem.

Curious about how Mom had been treated by the guests frequenting the beer garden, I asked her what she remembered about them.

"They were nice, ordinary people, dressed neat and clean even though they had been out working their farms. They liked to have a good time, talking about the harvest, the goings-on in town, and the war."

"How did they treat you?" I asked, wanting to know if they had been cruel or harsh because of her status as a slave worker, or because she was Slavic.

"They were polite, never getting angry if I didn't fill the beer fast enough—they kept me busy!" She paused, then continued, "They drank a lot of beer, but never got drunk or out of control."

I wondered if the guests were aware that less than thirty miles down the road innocent people were being tortured and slaughtered, or were they in denial? I couldn't imagine that ordinary people could have a good time while millions of people were suffering inconceivable pain and death.

The small Breitner farm only needed two forced laborers. Jozef's assignments included taking care of the horses, plowing the fields, and cutting hay with a sickle, while my mother milked and spread clean hay for the cows, hoed potatoes, harvested vegetables, cleaned the house, and served customers that frequented the beer garden.

Initially, the Breitners gave my mother physically undemanding work, plucking chickens and sewing grain sacks, since she had arrived at the farm weak and malnurished. After she regained her strength, her main job was milking the cows. Her hands swelled to twice their normal size during her first week of milking twelve cows, but the Breitners let her hands heal before requiring her to continue.

Mom slept in a cold storage room, down a long and dimly lit, narrow hallway from the kitchen. A rustic wood door opened to the cow barn, a few feet away. The room was drafty and not insulated. She spent many bitter cold nights in the storage room shivering under her thin blanket. Jozef slept in one of the upstairs bedrooms.

My mother said, "My first few weeks there, I often cried, and Jozef comforted me and helped me with my work whenever he could, lifting bales of hay and helping me carry the large buckets of milk into the house. He was such a gentleman, and he had a great sense of humor. If I got scared, nervous, or sad, he always cheered me up. The Breitners did not object to Jozef helping me with my chores, and they treated both of us cordially, but they showed more friendliness to Jozef. We had sufficient food to eat. The family ate in their restaurant and Jozef and I ate in the corner of the kitchen. Breakfast consisted of half a loaf of bread with jam, porridge and "speckle," a type of meat similar to bacon. Dinner was more substantial and included a large serving of *schnitzel* [a boneless meat cutlet], *kartoffel* [potatoes], vegetables, and dark rye bread with butter."

Jozef and my mother took turns walking to Wolnzach, less than two miles from the farm, to pick up the Breitner's mail. Employers allowed their forced laborers a small amount of freedom, which included socializing with other forced laborers on Sundays, but always under the watchful eye of German soldiers.

"Our clothes were tattered but Jozef was a meticulous dresser who brushed his clothes off whenever he finished his chores, and polished his boots at the end of each day. I admired his impeccable cleanliness," Mom told me.

During their time with the Breitners, the two of them developed a strong bond. Every Sunday morning, Jozef and a friend of his that he had known from the *stalag* walked to Gosseltshausen, where they spent leisure time with other forced laborers. One day his friend disappeared. Later, Jozef and my mother heard a rumor that the friend had become intimate with his employer's wife, and the two had planned on leaving Germany to be together after the war. The husband heard of the affair and transferred Jozef's friend immediately to Dachau for extermination. Jozef began walking to Gosseltshausen alone, but after a few weeks decided to invite my mother to accompany him.

As we sat on the couch on Mom's front porch while she recounted her life with Jozef in forced labor, her entire face suddenly lit up, a broad smile came over it, and she started to giggle, "I acted like a young schoolgirl going out on her first date!"

"Did you and Jozef hold hands when you walked to Gosseltshausen?" I asked, teasingly.

"No, he was a strict military man, it wouldn't have been proper for him to do that," she firmly responded.

"Did he compliment you, or tell you how much fun you were, that you were pretty, and he enjoyed being with you?" I wanted to know the details of how they fell in love.

"No, he was quiet, I'm sure he had a lot on his mind," but this time Mom's face looked puzzled.

I thought the scenario Mom had described a bit odd because men usually flatter women when they are trying to win their love, but I formed an image of Jozef as a highly disciplined, serious military man.

"I was thrilled to be walking by his side and dreamed of a future with him. I felt I had met my soulmate. After we got to know each other a little better, we talked about what we would do after the war. I wanted to return to Husne and open a cold-cuts store. Jozef planned to buy land and a few cows, but his plans changed constantly: sometimes he wanted to get married, have four sons, and work the farm; other times he told me he wanted to travel and see the world."

Mother always grew excited when she talked about Jozef and her on the Breitner farm, recalling those times as some of the happiest of her life. Gosseltshausen is where Jozef and my mother danced, sang, played cards, and talked about life after the war. Captured laborers from different countries all met at the same hall. They would dance and sing along to Polish songs played on an accordion in the large meeting room, but they had to leave before five in the afternoon, to return to the farm to milk the cows.

"Jozef loved to dance! You should have seen him dance the krakowiak! When he jumped and clicked his heels, everyone got excited—all eyes were on him! He was so smooth, yet electrifying to watch, and when he stamped his feet, I thought the floor would crash! He danced with all the women, and almost every dance. When everyone sang, he had the loudest, deepest voice that could be heard above all others. He was so enthusiastic, lively and energetic!" Mom said, her eyes sparkling.

I thought about what a sharp contrast that scene was to her previous description of Jozef being a quiet, highly disciplined military man who didn't hold her hand or have lively discussions with her.

• • •

The Breitners had three sons and two daughters. When the sons reluctantly left to fight for Germany, they hugged Jozef and my mother, and asked for their prayers. None of the Breitner children liked Hitler, except for their eldest daughter Hermania, who had a crush on Jozef and liked to sing Germany's national anthem, *"Deutschland, Deutschland, Uber Alles."*

Hermania excelled at mimicking the words and actions of the Gestapo and SS, barking orders to my mother at every opportunity.

"Jozef and I just laughed at Hermania's self-importance." Mom sang Germany's national anthem to me as she spoke of Hermania, laughing as she mimicked her voice.

Then her tone turned solemn. "Once, I tripped over a rock while carrying a bucket of milk. Outraged at the spilled milk and jealous of my friendship with Jozef, Hermania kicked me and then punched my face with her fist. When I fell down, she picked up a rock and started hitting me on the head with it. I had blood running down my face and Hermania kept screaming at me, cursing like a wild woman. A Nazi soldier heard her shrieking, and just as she was about to give me another blow to the head, he furiously ordered Hermania to stop. The soldier scared me; I thought he was going to shoot me, or send me back to Dachau, but when I heard him berate Hermania, I knew he was angry with her. No matter how I was treated by any of the Breitners, I would never risk showing animosity or disrespect toward them. I knew I could be beaten severely or sent back to the concentration camps for extermination."

Winters on the farm were brutal, Mom said, the windows always glazed thickly with ice. She remembers chopping wood one cold winter day, icicles hanging from her hair and face. Bone-chilling weather came in January and February, and she and Jozef were forced to chop wood in blinding blizzards. The Breitners gave them burlap potato bags to put over their shoes, but their feet became numb and frostbitten from the cold. They were never allowed to warm themselves by the fireplace.

Sometime during the war, the Third Reich notified the Breitners that all three of their sons had been killed. Mother could hear Frau Breitner wailing day and night, for months. After that, Frau Breitner treated Jozef and her with hostility, as if they were the cause of her sons' deaths.

I asked my mother to give me as much information as she had about her time in forced labor—names of people, places, and events, but the information came to me piecemeal and never with the details for which I desperately needed.

Mom had often told me about a close friend of hers who gave birth while in forced labor. With a faraway look, she narrated the account for me once more.

"My friend was made to leave the infant unattended during the day, while she worked in the field. She was only permitted to feed and change the baby during lunch. My friend could hear her baby crying from a distance, but could do nothing about it, for fear her employer would return her and the baby to the concentration camp, and they would be put to death. The German family was abusive with the infant and slapped the baby's head whenever it cried."

October 2006: Starzhausen, Germany

Starzhausen is located in the heart of the hops region of Germany, where mile after mile of the gently rolling hills are covered with the stalks of "green gold." The herbal aroma of hops—spicy, somewhat pungent—arouses an appetite to sit down with a smooth, cool, slightly foamy glass of beer. I felt like having a large glass of beer as we neared the Breitner house; I was beginning to feel a nervous adrenalin rush and needed to calm down.

The translator's eyes widened as I explained her assignment when we stopped down the street from the Breitner Guesthouse and Beer Garden. I had not told her or the driver the purpose of my trip.

When we pulled up to the house, I persuaded the translator to convince the Breitners to let me into their home and take pictures. I had been skeptical about being invited into the house. Several months prior to my trip to Germany, I had written to the Breitners, thanking them for taking good care of my mother and father while they were in forced labor. I let them know I planned on visiting and wanted to meet them, but I never received a response.

I felt apprehensive walking through the door of the Breitners' house, not knowing what to expect, thinking I would be rudely ordered out of the house. Liney Breitner greeted us, and welcomed us warmly when the translator explained who we were. She was the sole survivor of the Breitner estate and, despite her age, still operated the restaurant and beer garden.

Liney, a petite woman with clear grayish-blue eyes and neatly groomed silver hair pinned into an elegant bun, was stirring soup in a huge pot on the stove in the kitchen. She wore a spotless white linen hostess apron that had been tied in perfect bows at the back of her neck and waist. The large kitchen was equipped with massive white porcelain-enameled ovens with old-fashioned levered handles, six burners, a huge sink, and wide counters. The smell of boiling cabbage filled the room. I quickly surveyed the room, hoping to find the corner of the kitchen where Jozef and my mother had dined together, but the room did not have a small table and two chairs.

Liney remembered Jozef and my mother well, and smiled when she told me Jozef had stopped by several times to visit after the war. She didn't say much about Mother; Liney clearly liked Jozef, and spoke fondly of him, which made me feel proud that he was my father. She graciously allowed me to spend over an hour taking pictures of the house and beer garden. Returning to the kitchen, I saw Liney and my translator involved in a serious conversation, many questions and answers being conveyed. My translator looked concerned. During a pause in the conversation, I asked her what had been discussed. She groped for words, not making eye contact with me. I looked at her intently, waiting for her response. Finally, she said, "Your mother and father had a baby girl in 1944—she died at six weeks of age."

I was stunned and didn't know what to say. I must have mumbled something to them before walking out the door and into the forest.

Mom had never told me about this baby girl. I agonized for several weeks upon my return to the States. Should I question her about what must have been the most painful loss of her life—the death of her first-born? Was this the baby she had told me about, calling it her friend's baby, the infant who the German family hit on the head when she cried?

One day I found the courage to ask. I stared with disquiet when my mother nonchalantly said she knew nothing about this baby. I studied her face intensely for any clue about the poor baby girl, my sister, who was doomed so soon after her birth, but Mom's expression was blank. Perhaps it was too horrific for her to remember. There is no doubt in my mind that Liney Breitner had told the truth, nor would she have been confused about whose infant this was—she had a sharp mind and memory. I wanted my mother to revisit the pain of her loss, to heal her in some way, but her face revealed nothing and I have never mentioned it to her again. Her phlegmatic response to the death of her firstborn troubled me to the point that I forgot to ask her if she and Jozef had married while in forced labor, and if so, when, where, and how did he propose? I wanted to know the specific details as well as the factual data I could learn from their marriage certificate once I got a copy of it. I also sent my translator an email, asking her to contact Liney to get the baby's name and burial place, but never received a response.

• • •

When I returned from the forest, Liney was busy peeling potatoes for the guests that would be arriving soon. She excused herself, politely stating that she had to go back to work.

As we walked out, an elderly man introduced himself as Hermania's husband; he helped Liney operate the guesthouse. Despite the heat, he was dressed in a suit, vest, and tie, looking like an American business-man. A friendly, outgoing man, he asked if we needed any other infor-

Top: Forest across the street from Breitner guesthouse and farm where my mother helped an American pilot. Middle: Breitner homestead, Starzhausen, Germany. Above: The German people saluted Hitler's astonishing victories in the Breitner Restaurant, while Julia refilled their beer steins.

mation, but he did not know much about the war years on the farm since he and Hermania had married several years later.

I held my breath at the mention of Hermania, wanting to tell him the cruel story of what his wife had done to my mother. During my visit to Starzhausen, I hoped to meet Hermania, not knowing what I would say. Part of me wanted to lash out at her and I secretly hoped she had had a miserable life. Another part of me wanted to ask her, unemotionally, why she hurt my mother, and if she were sorry.

Hermania's husband and I exchanged pleasantries. Then I asked him about Hermania and he told me she had died a long time ago. My breathing stopped for an instant, and I hoped my face didn't reveal the conflict I felt. I could never confront Hermania's cruelty. In a way, I was relieved; I might break down at the sight of her. Mom had described Hermania as having a Gestapo face. Although it sounds callous, I took pleasure in knowing Hermania had been dead for many years, while my mother was still alive and enjoying life.

When we said goodbye to Hermania's husband, I shook his hand, and told him nothing of my feelings toward his late wife. As we took one last look at Starzhausen and the Breitner farm, I told the translator and driver what Hermania had done. They were appalled and I experienced a small sense of satisfaction in letting someone know about Hermania's mistreatment of my mother and how strong and brave she had been in the face of inhumanity.

FIVE

The War Ends

March 1945

Neither Jozef nor my mother knew anything of the Allied advances. The Breitners spoke in hushed tones, their conversations immediately stopping whenever Jozef and my mother entered the room. Their faces revealed fear and anger. Antoni became distant towards Jozef, no longer conferring with him on the military, or asking his advice on the care of the horses or the farmland. Gunfire and warplanes were heard more often, and working on the farm had become dangerous.

One day while working the far end of the field, Mother heard a siren, warning of an air attack. As soon as the drone of the engines became louder and dark images could be seen in the sky, she quickly took cover in a gully. German soldiers hiding in the forest began firing at the low-flying American planes. Caught in the crossfire, she stayed in the gully until the battle ended, face down in the muddy water, using a small boulder to protect her nose and mouth from the mud and debris rushing past her. She returned to the house frightened, dripping wet and dirty, but the Breitners only stared at her, not saying a word about her condition or asking if she had been hurt. Jozef didn't seem to be concerned either. Puzzled by her indifference toward his reaction, I asked her about it. She merely stated the war was ending and he had a lot on his mind. His reaction and her nonchalant response bothered me, yet I dismissed the warning sign. She continued her story about the time she spotted an American pilot parachuting to the ground and quickly ran towards him. The pilot raised his hand, shouting "Halt, Halt."

Mother quickly said, "Polish!"

The pilot, relieved, smiled, and she showed him a hiding place in the thick brush and conveyed with hand gestures that she would bring him food.

Safe on her porch in Denver, now an old woman, Mother recalled this story:

"Every day, I brought the pilot biscuits, meat, and milk, carefully concealed in my apron and I hid it in a hole of a hollowed tree in the forest. One day I discovered the American pilot had gone. He'd left a note, thanking me for my help and asking me to pray for him."

"If I survive the war," he wrote, "I will look for you."

"I never heard from him again."

I don't know in which language the note had been written, but Mom often told me this story, proud that she had helped an American soldier.

When Jozef and my mother first overheard conversations about Hitler attacking Russia and that America had entered the war, the implication of these events to their future was unclear. If Russia lost the war, they would be free from a centuries-old enemy; yet German rule would be no better. Their best chance for liberty and freedom depended on America.

German employers did not talk about how close the Americans were to their homes, and radios were kept at low volume. The Breitners looked at Jozef and Mother warily; they had been obedient and trustworthy workers for three years, but now that their freedom was imminent and the threat of being sent to the death camp could no longer be used to keep them in line, would they be able to control them?

The Breitners became less demanding of Jozef and Mother, no longer having an interest in maintaining the farm and house. Their entire focus was on the outcome of the war, and what the consequences to them would be. They hoped America, not Russia, would occupy their homeland. Russia, they knew, would show no mercy to the German people. They believed they would get significantly better treatment from America.

Still, Jozef and my mother feared their lives were in danger now that they would no longer be needed. Would German soldiers rush into their rooms and shoot them in one final attempt to destroy the enemy or the evidence of war crimes?

"I was afraid and wanted Jozef to comfort and reassure me, but Jozef became annoyed with me. He was restless and agitated because the end of the war was taking too long. Sometimes I thought he would just walk out of the house—he wanted his freedom more than anything, and his edginess made me nervous. I used to enjoy our quiet evening meals in the kitchen corner, but now Jozef just stared at the wall, drumming his fingers on the table and then quickly going upstairs to his room," Mom said. I felt a knot in my stomach.

While three million Allied troops staged the Normandy landing on June 6, 1944—the largest amphibious invasion in all of history—Jozef and my mother continued their forced labor on the Breitner farm, unaware that freedom was getting closer. Mother sensed the tide of the war had changed for Germany. Guests at the Breitner beer garden no longer laughed or toasted the Fuhrer; instead, a nervous, somber quiet pervaded the large room, which was now more than half empty.

Normandy changed the course of the war. The battle at Normandy began with the Allies parachuting behind enemy lines, followed by massive air attacks and naval bombardments the next day. For more than two months, the battle raged. By its conclusion, 210,000 Allied and 215,000 German soldiers had been killed.

Hitler understood the consequences of Normandy, stating, "In the East, the vastness of space will permit a loss of territory, without suffering a mortal blow to Germany's chance for survival. Not so in the West! If the enemy here succeeds, consequences of staggering proportions will follow within a short time."

After the Normandy victory, the Allies pushed toward the Rhine River, their next strategic target. Hitler's hope for victory depended on preventing the enemy from crossing it into Germany. It was to be held at all costs. As the Allied Forces approached the river in December 1944, Hitler's troops followed his command to demolish all bridges and blew them up.

Hitler orders the destruction of bridges on the Rhine River to prevent the Allies from entering Germany, circa 1945.

By the end of March 1945, the legendary Rhine River, which had prevented Julius Caesar's conquest of Germania and had served to protect Germany from its enemies for over two thousand years, had been breached, leading to the country's inevitable defeat. Not all of the bridges had been successfully demolished in time, enabling the Allies to smash their way across the Rhine and invade Western Germany.

As the Allied Forces invaded Germany from the west, the Red Army regrouped from the east and captured German-occupied territories, charging through Hungary to Poland and Austria. When the Russian army neared Berlin, Hitler ordered all available soldiers, civilian males between the ages of twelve and sixty-five, to defend Berlin to their deaths. He then took shelter in his underground bunker.

• • •

Everything became eerily quiet inside the Breitner house. Laughter from the beer garden could no longer be heard. Antoni and Frau Breitner's faces revealed a controlled despair. Still grieving the loss of her sons, Frau Breitner became a recluse in her bedroom, seldom making an appearance to manage the household. The responsibility fell on Hermania, who by now privately sang *"Deutschland, Deutschland, Uber Alles"* as if it were a funeral hymn. She became friendly toward my mother, treating her with kindness for the first time, fearing Mother might report her to American authorities.

One evening Hermania came to the barn where Mother sat on a stool milking a cow. Looking at the bucket of milk reminded her of the day she had brutally smashed my mother's face with a rock for having spilled the milk. Mother looked up at Hermania cautiously, but Hermania had a frightened, desperate look on her face, and she nervously begged my mother not to say anything to the Americans, explaining she didn't know why she did it, and that she was sorry.

Mom told me that she had responded, "Only God can judge you."

"I wonder if Hermania would have apologized so profusely if Germany had won the war," I said.

My mother had been in forced labor for three years when the war was about to end. She had adjusted to her life in slavery, and in many ways felt it was not much different from her childhood in Husne. Being near Jozef offset the negative aspects of her life in captivity.

Jozef, on the other hand, became increasingly restless, knowing he would soon be free. He refused to talk about the future with my mother; she could think of nothing else, and began envisioning her new life with him.

One day Antoni ordered Jozef to hitch the horses to their large wagon so they could swiftly transport as many German soldiers as possible to Berlin for their last stand. Jozef was gone for several weeks, and my mother feared he had been killed or captured.

Relieved to see Jozef when he returned, my mother ran to him with outstretched arms, and was surprised when he quickly turned away.

"Why do you think that was?" I asked Mom.

She stated, a little too casually, "Jozef was a highly disciplined military man who knew the horses were his first priority."

It didn't ring true to me, and I surmised that Mom was in denial about the meaning of Jozef's dismissive, distancing behavior.

On April 24, the Red Army surrounded Berlin and the siege continued for more than a week, with heavy fighting and house-to-house combat. By the time Berlin surrendered on May 2, 1945, 305,000 Soviet soldiers and 325,000 Germans had died in this battle. Berlin was looted, ransacked, and over 100,000 women were raped by Soviet troops.

Knowing defeat and capture were imminent, Hitler married his long-time mistress, Eva Braun, and then committed suicide with her in his underground bunker, located under the garden of the Reichskanzlei.

On May 7, 1945, one week after Hitler's suicide, Germany unconditionally surrendered to the Allies. Europe celebrated Victory in Europe Day (V-E) on May 8. With the death of Hitler and the destruction of Berlin, the Third Reich was completely defeated.

Jozef and my mother heard shots being fired throughout Starzhausen at war's end. A little more than thirty minutes before the first American soldiers arrived in the town, the SS had been hiding in the Breitner's cow barn, covered with straw, and the upstairs bedrooms of the house. When they heard the shots, the soldiers fled; the Breitner family hurriedly took cover in the basement, allowing Jozef and my mother shelter in it as well.

My mother recalled, "The American soldiers entered the restaurant shouting, 'Come up with your hands up!' The Breitners ordered me to take a white cloth and forced me to be the first to surrender. Shaking in fear, I could barely walk up the narrow and steep steps of the basement. Everything seemed to be in slow motion, but I remember when I came to the top of the stairs, I started yelling, as loud as possible, 'Polish! Polish!' and I feverishly waved the white flag. When the American soldiers saw me, they proclaimed, 'You are free!'"

SIX

Displaced Persons

Thirty-eight years had gone by since I first learned Jozef was my father and I had successfully traced him from Deblin to Moosburg, and Starzhausen. I thought the remaining research, the period between the defeat of Germany and our arrival in America, would be easy. All I would need is the list of displaced persons, and track his movements. But tracing Jozef and Mother's footsteps after the war became a formidable mission. The victors divided and occupied four areas in Germany, establishing DP camps in each of their zones. DP records had been transferred to many organizations including the successor agency to the United Nations Relief and Rehabilitation Agency (UNRRA), the International Refugee Organization (IRO). The IRO records were transferred to the National Archives and Records Administration, and had been destroyed many years ago.

I continued to look at the stars of the night sky, wondering when, or if, I would ever find Jozef. He had disappeared somewhere in those DP camps and they could hold the answer I was seeking. I began researching life as a displaced person, not only because I might stumble across a vital clue that could help me find Jozef, but also as a way I could empathize with him. On a deeper level, I wanted to explain to that twelve-year-old boy who contemptuously yelled "Dirty DPs" to me during Mother's proud moment of becoming an American citizen that we were not vagrants seeking a gratis life in the United States. Our homelands had been taken away from us and we were the people in Emma Lazarus' famous poem, engraved on the pedestal on which the Statue of Liberty stands:

Not like the brazen giant of Greek fame,
With conquering limbs astride from land to land;
Here at our sea-washed, sunset gates shall stand
A mighty woman with a torch, whose flame
Is the imprisoned lightning, and her name
Mother of Exiles. From her beacon-hand
Glows world-wide welcome; her mild eyes command
The air-bridged harbor that twin cities frame.
"Keep, ancient lands, your storied pomp!" cries she
With silent lips. "Give me your tired, your poor,
Your huddled masses yearning to breathe free,
The wretched refuse of your teeming shore.
Send these, the homeless, tempest-tost to me,
I lift my lamp beside the golden door!

My journey into the DP camps began with an academic research of the UNRRA's arduous mission of organizing an orderly exodus from Germany and ended with learning disquieting, heart-wrenching secrets.

Providing food and shelter for millions of refugees was the first priority of the UNRRA. Former German military centers, concentration camps, barracks, and sometimes an entire village or section of a city were employed to house the refugees. Hospitals, hotels, castles, private homes, and even partially destroyed buildings were also put into service. At first, shelter was improvised and those in charge would even share their food, clothing, and supplies. As the UNRRA became more organized, clothing drives were held in Australia, New Zealand, Canada, and the United States. With the threat of a typhoid epidemic

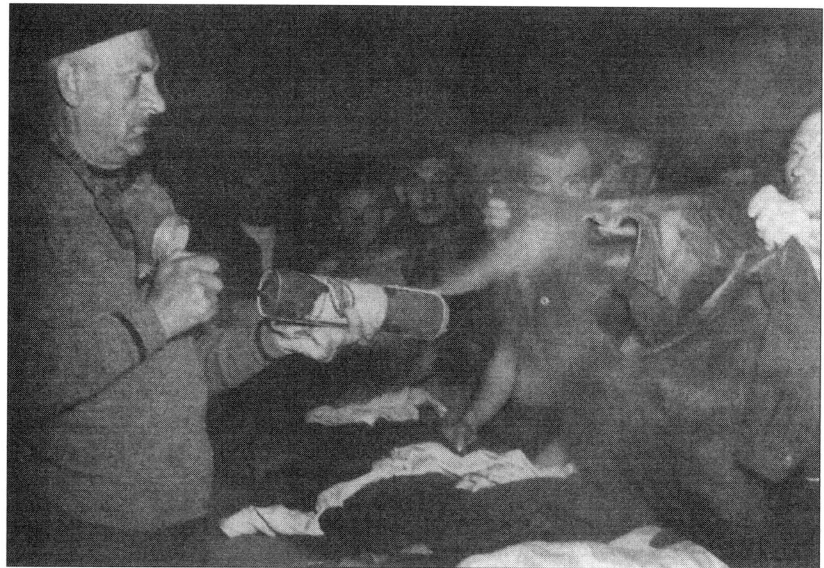

Lice-infested refugees get sanitized with DDT, 1945.

looming from the lice-infested refugees, the UNRRA began dusting the DPs with DDT.

Displaced persons languished in camps in Germany for two years following WWII. When violence erupted in the camps, the over-crowded DP situation came to international attention and countries began opening their doors. South American countries were the first to accept refugees, followed by Australia, Canada, Great Britain, Belgium, and France. Jozef could have ended up in any one of the dozens of countries around the globe. He had an adventuress spirit and had informed my mother of his desire to travel the world, so he may have abandoned us to fulfill his dream.

America initially refused to allow entry of Europe's DPs, but Christian organizations lobbied Congress and the White House, and displaced persons were finally permitted entry, on the condition that sponsoring organizations would guarantee housing and jobs for the emigrants.

The United States was, in fact, the last country to open its doors. Finally, on July 7, 1947, President Harry S. Truman stated that, "It is unthinkable that displaced persons should be left indefinitely in camps in Europe."

America meant freedom, opportunity, and the realization of hopes and dreams, especially to displaced persons whose experiences during the war and desperation to start over intensified their drive for a new life. That primal drive is illustrated in the tragic story about two daughters and their blind father trying to immigrate to America, as told by Mark Wyman in his book *DPs: Europe's Displaced Persons, 1945–1951*. The family was repeatedly rejected for immigration because of the father's blindness. As the 1951 deadline for permission to immigrate approached, the daughters were finally accepted, but the father was not. The daughters refused to leave without their father, so in order for them to be free to go to America he hung himself.

Many refugees moved from camp to camp, searching for lost family members, fellow countrymen, or hoping to find better food and accommodations. Within the DP camps, refugees naturally clustered by nationality and religion. As the UNRRA issued registration cards, all were transported to camps, organized by nationality and religion to minimize conflicts and language barriers.

Housing consisted of overcrowded barracks that provided little privacy. The many children born and growing up in the camps were educated in makeshift schools. People stood in line for food rations, and cooked and washed outdoors. Their time was spent doing chores, playing cards, and drinking. Employment opportunities were rare.

Over the next six years, the displaced persons camps became home to two million refugees. The camps evolved into little communities, and the DPs attended improvised churches in fields, basements, and even horse stables. Newspapers sprang up. Many prepared for a better future by enrolling in the Displaced Persons University, established in Munich in 1946, which offered a full curriculum of courses. Refugee musicians formed orchestras and performed open-air concerts. Children were given music lessons using donated instruments. Sporting events were organized. People's lives changed dramatically waiting for word on what would become of them.

In the limited privacy of the barracks, the refugees spoke in hushed tones of shocking and disquieting secrets. Many tried to forget the hundreds of babies buried in unmarked graves in the camps' fields. The cause of death for the newborns—whether disease, malnutrition, or because they were abandoned—will never be known. As I researched DP camps, I learned that my mother was not alone: most parents would not talk about that time in their lives. It was not until my mother was in her eighties and I had spent a lifetime doing research that Mom became more open to talking.

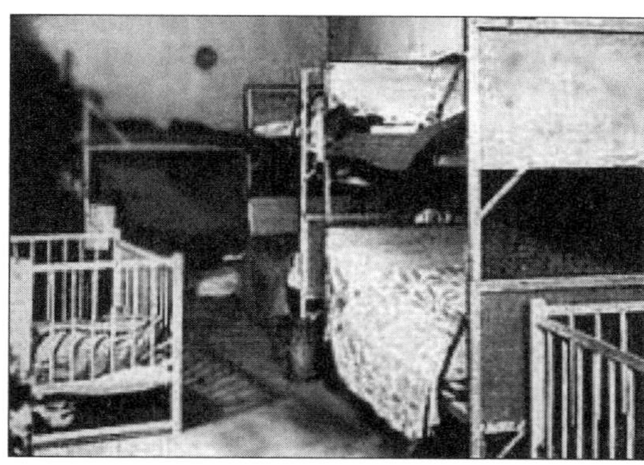

Top: Displaced persons queued for food rations, 1945.
Center: Cooking at the Displaced Persons Center, 1945–51.
Bottom: The cramped interior of the Displaced Persons Center, 1945–51.

My front porch conversations with Mom now turned to her life with Jozef in the displaced persons camps.

"Every day of our years as prisoners in Germany, Jozef and I dreamed we would be free to return to Poland. We were in our late twenties when the war ended, still young enough to rebuild our lives. We had three options: Stay in Germany and continue to work for the Breitners, as they had offered; return to Poland; or immigrate to a new country. America was our first choice. Jozef talked about returning to his hometown, reclaiming a portion of his land, and building a small house. I thought about going back to Husne and opening a cold-cuts store, reclaiming the property I had inherited from Oluzia." Mother's statements about her and Jozef's future plans clearly showed me they had decided to part ways.

"Being freed by the Americans was what we had been praying for and everyone rejoiced, but the exhilaration was short-lived. We heard that the 'Big Three' leaders—Josef Stalin, Winston Churchill, and Franklin Roosevelt—came to an agreement in Yalta that the Soviet Union could retain its influence over the countries it occupied."

Stalin's goal to divide Germany and claim Eastern Europe for the Soviet Union had been achieved. Churchill admitted the enormity of the judgment errors made at Yalta in a speech in Fulton, Missouri, March 5, 1946, when he uttered the famous line, "... an Iron Curtain has descended across the continent."

"We were shocked to learn that our homeland would remain under Soviet rule. We feared Stalin, and heard reports of executions and mass deportations to Siberia. Stalin began deporting retired Polish officers and intelligentsia almost immediately."

Mother talked with me quietly about how Jozef started to worry that returning to Poland would be dangerous. "Jozef became restless and agitated staying at the Breitner farm. Every day, he saw truckloads of refugees driving by the guesthouse, being transported to the DP camps. Day and night, we saw hundreds of refugees going to the camps. Many walked barefoot, wearing rags or mismatched military uniforms. Some of them looked like skeletons, close to death.

"Millions of people were taking advantage of their freedom and wanted to start a new life. Although Jozef and Antoni were friends, he

Displaced persons begin returning to their homelands, or to refugee camps at war's end, circa 1945.

knew that unless he married one of the Breitner daughters, he would never own the property. And, once the war was over and German soldiers began returning home, Hermania cooled toward Jozef and set her sights on marrying a German.

"Jozef talked to me about both of us relocating to a refugee camp, where we could submit our applications for immigration to America." Mom's eyes glowed as she relayed to me her pleasure that Jozef was including her in his future plans.

"Didn't it bother you that Jozef considered marrying Hermania so he could own the Breitner property, and that now that she had lost interest in him, he turned his attention to you?" I asked.

Mom said nothing for several moments, then continued, "Jozef talked to officials about his desire to immigrate to the U.S., and that the DP camps had a reputation of being overcrowded and the food was just rations of pre-packaged meals. The UNRRA assured Jozef there was sufficient room and asked him if he'd be willing to be one of the camp's leaders, who acted as liaisons between the refugees and the UNRRA." She was clearly proud that Jozef had been asked to be the camp leader.

The position would entitle my parents to a private room at the Pfaffenhofen camp, so Jozef accepted the offer and, with my mother, boarded the next UNRRA truck that came to Starzhausen bound for Pfaffenhofen.

My mother and Jozef arrived in August of 1945 at the Pfaffenhofen camp. It was located on the outskirts of town, away from the general population. The UNRRA, with help from local Germans, hastily constructed barracks from freshly cut timber and corrugated tin. A little over four thousand people lived in Pfaffenhofen during the 1940s, but the town doubled in size with the influx of displaced persons.

My mother told me, "The locals didn't like having the camp in their impeccable and quaintly historic town. They referred to us as *auslanders* [foreigners] and insisted we stay confined to the isolated area of Pfaffenhofen. We were not allowed to use their churches, schools, or hospital."

Although given more freedom in the DP camps than on the Breitner farm, it was not altogether unrestricted there. Initially, Jozef relished in his role as the camp leader and kept busy with organizational and administrative matters, settling disputes and making decisions. He also enjoyed the benefits of their private room, which was close to the administrative building and convenient for meeting with other DPs and UNRRA officials.

Mother said, "Jozef's strong presence enabled him to be an effective liaison for the UNRRA but he soon returned to his old feelings of being agitated and restless. He grew tired of settling petty squabbles of the camp's residents. He was almost thirty years old by then and he started to feel that the UNRRA assignment would not provide any significant opportunities for him. He told me he wanted to get on with his life, but I had no idea what he meant by that."

From what I could gather by listening to Mom talk, it was apparent that at first she was oblivious to the changes in Jozef's behavior.

Mom said, "At the Breitner farm Jozef had been polite, helpful, obedient, and he had a sense of humor. Now he was sullen and angry and he had violent outbursts. Even the rain on the tin roof unnerved him!

But I was in love with him and overlooked many things. I wanted to get married but he dismissed the idea whenever I brought up the subject. Then I became pregnant."

Mom sadly told me about Jozef's refusal to marry her when she informed him she was pregnant, and this was the first time that I was forced to question my fantasies about my father's heroic character. I considered the reasons my father might have refused to marry my mother: he didn't love her; the responsibility of a wife and child would prevent him from pursuing his dreams; he was already married?

As their daughter, I wanted a love story. If Jozef didn't love my mother, then why didn't he leave her at the Breitner farm? I imagined that he must have had feelings for her and that a bond did exist between them. Perhaps there was something deep within him that he could not overcome to marry her? I concluded that I would only know the answer when I found him.

Within nine months of Jozef's and Mother's arrival in Pfaffenhofen, my older sister Krystyna was born in the camp hospital, a barrack that had been converted to treat injuries and illnesses of the DPs. Camp hospital supplies and equipment included only minimum essential inventory and first aid items, and provided little real medical treatment. When it came time to deliver, she was not given medication nor did a doctor come for the delivery; a midwife from the DP camp assisted.

My sister Krystyna, age thirteen months, Pfaffenhoffen, Germany, 1947.

Mom was visibly upset but she seemed open to telling me this long-held story. "Jozef wanted a son and Krystyna's birth angered him. He demanded that I not record his name as the father on the birth registration. I was devastated by his reaction but didn't pressure him. I hoped the kind and gentle Jozef I had known on the Breitner farm would reemerge, and he would realize he loved me and want to marry me and accept our baby."

The news that Jozef did not want his name on Krystyna's birth certificate disturbed me. The only explanation I could imagine was that Jozef already had a wife and children in Poland. I began fantasizing that he was a distinguished military commander whose reputation would be destroyed if word leaked out that he had fathered a child, and that the birth certificate could be used as proof against him.

October 2003: Pfaffenhofen, Germany

During my search for my father, I discovered eight towns named Pfaffenhofen in Germany. The particular Pfaffenhofen where the DP camp was established is about thirty-five miles north of Munich.

My husband Keith and I left Munich mid-morning and arrived in Pfaffenhofen a half-hour later. Smoke billowed from the train as it came to a slow stop in front of the three-story, tangerine-colored station. As we stepped onto the platform, Keith pointed out an abandoned, small, two-story, dark brown brick building with elaborate white window frames that had probably been used as the station during WWII.

I thought of my mother standing in front of this building, waiting to be taken to her next destination. Keith and I walked up twenty metal steps, over the bridge, and down the steps on the other side to the tangerine-colored building. At the main entrance, we found one taxi in the small parking lot in front. It was a cool, overcast day, and I hoped it wouldn't rain. I could smell the dankness of hops in the air.

As we headed toward the city center, I marveled at the clean and well-maintained buildings. The city's storefronts had been painted in pastel pink, blue, and green; the broad sidewalks were made from light brown pavers. When the taxi turned left toward the main street, I noticed a large sign: "Breitner." It was a bakery, and I realized that until that moment I'd been spelling the name as it would have been spelled in English: Brightner.

Large trees divided the main street, which ended at the municipal building, a three-story white masonry building with a black-tiled gabled roof. A bell tower with a sharp, pointed steeple was at the building's center, the entrance to the formidable building. The cab driver dropped us off in front of the city office, the most dominant building in Pfaffenhofen, a ten-minute drive from the train station. My excitement turned to disappointment when I found the Information Office door locked. I peered down dimly lit hallways, but no city employees were in sight.

I stood in the middle of the large foyer of the city office and my thoughts about what to do next were interrupted by the loud chatter of young people descending an immense staircase. I asked a teenage boy where the registry office was located, and he directed me to the third floor. Two giggling teenage girls came running down the stairs as we ascended, and we overheard the boy excitedly say, "Americans! Americans!"

On the third floor, we again found ourselves looking down long dimly lit hallways, the massive doors all closed. We knocked on each door as we made our way down the hallway, growing more leery with each unanswered knock. Finally, a young woman opened the last door in the corridor.

She spoke English relatively well, and understood that I was asking about my sister's birth registration. I wanted to confirm the date and time of Krystyna's birth, as well as unearth any other information regarding my mother or Jozef.

My mother had always claimed that Krys and I had both been born on the exact same date: Krys at noon and me at midnight, two years apart. I believed this story up until 1961 when I had discovered Jozef was my biological father. I knew Mom was an honest person, but I became suspicious of any factual data concerning me and Jozef since the time of that revelation.

The young woman explained Germany's privacy rules and asked to see my passport, and proof that Krystyna was my sister. I told her that I didn't bring any written evidence, but I could tell her the date of birth and our mother's name. The registry assistant hesitated and then deferred to her supervisor, a man of about forty, dressed in a suit and tie, sitting behind a large wooden desk in the far corner of the office. He looked at my passport, surveyed me quickly, and nodded. I smiled thanks.

A handwritten note on the far right side of Krystyna's birth registration stated that Paul Venckus had adopted Krystyna and given her his name. Paul was the man I had always called my father; it was a strange feeling to come upon his name in this faraway land where I had come in search of my biological father.

While I studied the document, a side conversation in German took place between the registry assistant and her supervisor. When it ended, she happily informed me that, although nearly all the DP barracks had been demolished decades before, incredibly the one in which Jozef and my mother had lived still existed. She said it was within walking distance and could give me directions. I reached in my purse, asking the amount of the fee. The young woman smiled and replied, "No charge."

I asked the registry assistant, who had clearly become interested in my story, if records or lists of the DPs who had passed through Pfaffenhofen existed. She believed that the UNRRA had taken all of them, and the city did not have a duplicate set. She accompanied us out of the office, asking if we wanted to see the city chambers. Having been in many city chambers in the United States, I was curious to see a German one and the registry assistant seemed to want to take us on a tour of Pfaffenhofen's proud history.

Top: Pfaffenhofen City Council Chambers, 2006. Above: Apartment complex in Pfaffenhofen that I mistook for former displaced persons camp.

Pfaffenhofen's city chambers were designed in much the same way as city chambers in the United States, with the notable exception of the large oil paintings of Bavarian kings hanging on the walls. Smiling with pride, the registry assistant told us the name of each Bavarian king.

We stopped by the Burgermeister's (mayor's) office, which displayed photographs of previous mayors, and were given a packet of information on Pfaffenhofen. As we walked and talked, the assistant appeared genuinely happy that we had come from America to visit her city and she went out of her way to be helpful.

On our own now, on Ingolstadter Strasse, Keith and I recognized the car dealership that the registry assistant had informed us was near the DP barracks. The adjacent apartments had possibly been converted, though I had envisioned DP housing as resembling U.S. Army barracks:

austere but not ramshackle. I didn't know which of the apartments my mother and father might have lived in so I snapped pictures of all of them. Once I got back to Denver, I planned to show them to Mom and see if she could recognize the place in history where she once lived.

My picture taking caused quite a stir in the apartment complex! Residents pulled back curtains, puzzled and disconcerted. A middle-aged man with a neatly trimmed beard and moustache, dressed in blue jeans and a crisply starched blue-plaid shirt, came out and asked us in heavy broken English and a friendly tone, "May I help you with something?"

I pulled the birth registration from the large packet and pointed to the address on the document. The man looked puzzled. "This is written in very old German, and I can't read it. Please come upstairs, and I will show it to my mother, who can."

The tidy apartment did not have a couch and the furniture resembled 1950s American design: straight lines with no elaborate carving. Two slightly stuffed chairs sat behind the coffee table and each of the remaining three wooden straight-backed chairs had end tables beside them. Hummels and other German knickknacks were placed on top.

The man's wife and young son stood near his mother and scrutinized us. He handed the older woman the document and they began conversing in German. The mother was insulted! We had mistaken her apartment for DP barracks, which were further down the street, beyond the Weber auto dealership. The name "Weber" jolted my memory and I had to agree with the woman that we were in the wrong place.

Keith and I thanked the family profusely and apologized for disrupting their afternoon. As we left, the man told us that his mother was certain that the person who had signed the document was still alive, his memory was good, and he could give us more information.

We eventually found the dilapidated barracks in a blighted part of town. Portions of the barracks were fenced off and had waist-high weeds. It was obvious that German authorities wanted to restrict access to it. My mind grew full of wild thoughts that the building contained a terrible secret and I told myself to stop preposterous notions. Suddenly, I wanted to jump the fence and go inside. But something held me back. I looked at the tall weeds, fearful, envisioning snakes slithering across my feet or rats jumping on me. The building might collapse on us.

By now it was dusk and I stood staring at the barrack in which Jozef and my mother had lived over fifty years ago. It looked foreboding and I didn't want to go inside, afraid I would not be able to re-emerge. Would Jozef's ghost come out of a dark corner and do something to me? I had traveled thousands of miles to get to this place, but now I couldn't move one inch. I knew if I went inside, I might fall to pieces. I wanted to cry because I didn't have the courage to go inside that barrack, but I pulled myself together, thinking Keith might worry I'd gone off the deep end. I took out my camera, hands shaking, and started snapping pictures.

My mother and father (Jozef) lived in this DP barrack from 1945 to 1947, Pfaffenhoffen, Germany.

Looking back, my decision not to enter the barrack is one I'll regret for the rest of my life. I will never know what it felt like to be in the place where Jozef and my mother lived, or visualize their young lives together. Distraught with myself for not being able to enter the barrack, I forgot about the old man who had a good memory and could tell me something about Jozef. Thinking about all this still saddens me. In my mind I can hear the word *auslanders,* Jozef's angry outbursts, and feel my mother's pain and despair at Jozef's rejection of the birth of their beautiful daughter.

I wished I could meet my father and tell him about his daughter Krystyna, and that she likes to sing and dance as he once did. I wanted him to know that Krys had graduated cum laude and was a successful businesswoman. She has two smart daughters with successful careers. His granddaughter Michele graduated from college summa cum laude, and Lisa was in school to become a veterinarian. They are happy and friendly people. I wanted so much to see Jozef's smile as we talked about his daughter Krystyna and her family.

As Keith and I slowly walked back to Pfaffenhofen's city center, my mind kept saying, "Go back!" but by now it was dark and I grew more frightened of entering the haunted barrack. Before hailing a cab, Keith and I stopped at a general merchandise store, where I bought a souvenir for Krys: a beer stein with a picture of Pfaffenhofen as it had been in ancient times.

I was beginning to get a little nervous about the ending to this story. Would it be in any way happy? My next stop, Altenstadt, the place of my birth and where Jozef disappeared, would take me closer to an answer.

• • •

Castle of Bavarian King Ludwig II, Neuschwanstein, Germany.

My mother had told me that I was born in Altenstadt, Bavaria, where King Ludwig II built his fairy tale castle, the one Walt Disney recreated for his Disneyland.

When I traveled through Germany, I found the country to be majestic, with lush rolling hills, small villages of red-tile roofed houses, and magnificent castles atop flower-covered mountains. I tried to envision a war-ravaged Germany, as it had been when Jozef and my mother had lived there—a country in ruins, charred trees marring the once green landscape, dilapidated buildings and houses that had fallen into disrepair, their windows caked with dust and grime.

As we drove by the Papstliche Basilica, I remembered Eckhart had advised me to check church records for my birth information, but when I had asked Mom for the name of the church where I was baptized, she told me DPs were not allowed to christen their children in Germany's churches; the sacrament had been performed in one of the barracks, demolished decades ago. Seeing the noble church saddened me as I thought about how difficult it must have been for Mother, who had strong religious convictions, to not be allowed to baptize her children in a church.

Papstliche Basilica, Altenstadt, Germany.

Two years prior to the invasion of Poland, Germany's unified armed forces, known as the Wehrmacht, built a command post in an outlying area north of Altenstadt, which the UNRRA converted after the war to a DP camp. Pinpointing the location of Altenstadt was a major research project for me, as German maps listed five different Altenstadts. To complicate things, "Altenstadt" means "old town" in German, and almost every municipality, city, town, or village in Germany has a section of town named Altenstadt. It took me nearly two months of emailing German archives to zero in on the Altenstadt near Schongau as the correct place of my birth.

When I had mentioned Schongau to Mom, a sad and distant look came across her face as she recalled the story of my birth. "After transferring from Pfaffenhoffen to Altenstadt, Jozef and I settled into new barracks, but our daily life didn't change. We continued the same routines: me cooking, cleaning, washing, and caring for little Krystyna, and Jozef playing cards and drinking. During the evenings, refugees gathered around tables, talking about the future. On one of those cool summer nights Jozef told me, 'None of us knows where we will end up, but I want you to know that I will always remember you.'"

ALTENSTADT DP CENTER

UNRRA TEAM 150
APO 757 U. S. ARMY

TELEPHONE SCHONGAU 212,
307, 381, 388

DATE April 26, 1946

No. 127.

TO Landrat Schongau
FROM UNRRA Team 150
SUBJECT: Requisition

20 Poles - Stangen 7 m lang, ø- 10 - 12 cm.

Raymond D. BELL
Supply Officer
UNRRA Team 150

Top: Entrance papers to Altenstadt Displaced Persons Center, April 26, 1946. Above: Former Wehrmacht compound (Unified Armed Forces of Nazi Germany) converted to refugee camp, 1946.

I stared at my mother, wondering how she must have felt hearing those words and realizing Jozef envisioned the rest of his life without her.

"The war was over and I felt Jozef starting to distance himself. But I chose to close my eyes to obvious signs."

When my mother quietly informed Jozef that she was pregnant again, he briefly became more demonstrative and loving. She was ecstatic when he agreed to marry her. They completed a marriage license application and were about to send it off to Schongau.

"But Jozef grew sullen," my mother said, "and ripped up the application one night in a fit of rage. I was devastated but accepted his cruelty, because I believed he would change."

It is hard to know whether, if circumstances had been different, how my mother's life—and my own—might have turned out some other way. As Mom rocked on her Denver porch, her face wrinkled with age, I heard her tell two stories of seemingly random events that forever changed us.

Mom was reminiscing about both the good and hard parts of her time in Altenstadt. "Stanislaw Sadovski was one of Jozef's inner circle of friends at the camp. They played cards with a number of other men and often returned late at night. In the early morning hours one day, after playing cards all night long, Stanislaw took a shortcut and crossed the railroad tracks on the way back to the barracks. It was still dark and he saw the brakeman preparing to connect two cars, but thought he could make it. As he darted across, he was halfway when the cars connected and severed his legs! He survived, but it was extremely painful for Jozef to see his good friend, who had survived the horrors of Nazism, lose his legs in a freak accident. Jozef pulled away and became morose. I couldn't reach him."

Another Polish couple, Jozef Walczek and his girlfriend Julie, lived on the opposite side of the barrack from my mother and Jozef. They were best friends, helping each other with household chores and childcare. According to Mom, "Julie was a beautiful young woman with large blue eyes and a strong personality who loved to flirt with the men."

Jozef Walczek was married to another woman and had children back in Poland, but he lived with Julie at the camp and they had four daughters of their own. Like many other DPs, Jozef Walczek decided not to return to a Communist-ruled Poland, thereby deserting his former family. Such choices were not uncommon, and many children of displaced persons have been shocked to discover that they have half-siblings on the other side of the globe. The circumstances that led to such abandonments are almost impossible to fathom, and yet there are so many who must live with these stories as part of their family history and legacy.

Mother told me, "In early fall of 1948, Jozef Walczek went deer hunting in a nearby forest in Altenstadt. Either he didn't see the posted "No Trespassing" sign or he ignored it, but when a German police officer ordered him to "Halt," he did not, and the German patrol shot him. Walczek lived several hours with your father attending to his needs. As he lay dying, Walczek begged him to take care of his Julie and their four daughters."

At the time, my mother could not have known that this deathbed promise would result in the next great upheaval of her life.

"I assumed that everyone in the DP camp would unite to look after Julie and the children. But the day after Jozef Walczek died, your father left us and moved in with Julie and her four girls."

Mom's revelation shocked me: My father had left us for another woman. I had wanted a dramatic, heart-wrenching reason for Jozef's abandonment, not a cliché.

My father's new residence was located on the opposite side of the barrack, but my mother could clearly see him with Julie and her children. She vividly remembers the pain she felt watching Jozef carrying one of Julie's daughters in his arms and holding the other's hand, something she longed for him to do with his own children. Whenever Jozef and my mother

Above: Altenstadt Displaced Persons Center, 1948. My sister Krystyna is second from right.
Left: Altenstadt Displaced Persons Center, 1948. That's me in the arms of my godparents.

made eye contact, Jozef quickly turned away. He no longer provided for us; any extra food that he once gave to us went to his new family.

Jozef's abandonment of my mother was the scandal of Altenstadt DP camp. Antoni and Janka Mucha, friends to both Jozef and Mother, sided with my mother and confronted Jozef many times, but their interference only angered him. Enamored by Julie, he refused to return to my mother. Friends in the camp tried to console her and brought her extra food, emotional support, showed her special attention, and invited her to their barrack for activities that would help to keep her mind off Jozef. But my mother had a broken heart and became despondent.

"You and Krys were the only joy in my life," my mother said.

It is difficult for me to imagine this vibrant, energetic, daring woman who had survived the terror of Dachau being mistreated in this way.

Not only was her heart broken, she felt humiliated by the stares and whispers wherever she went in the camp. Finally, the UNRRA transferred Jozef, Julie, and the four young daughters to a different barrack.

Almost sixty years later, Mom cried as she described seeing Jozef holding Walczek's baby girl. Wiping her eyes she asked me to try to find Julie Walczek.

"I would like to ask my former friend why she stole Jozef away from me."

I told her, "When someone truly loves a person, no one can steal him away."

My mother became quiet, staring into the night sky.

October 2003: Altenstadt, Germany

As the train rambled through small villages en route to Altenstadt, I spotted a Shetland pony and a few contented deer in the lush green forests. I had traveled this far to visit the site of my birth and to solve two major mysteries: the exact date I was born, and my father's next destination after Altenstadt, information I considered essential for retracing his steps from the time of his disappearance.

I had a birth certificate issued by the International Refugee Organization, which allowed me to immigrate to the U.S. Issued two years after my birth, it named Paul Venckus as my father. I wanted to see my original birth certificate, to confirm the date and to see if Jozef Kurek had been identified as my father.

By the time the train screeched to a stop at the Schongau station, it had started to rain lightly. As my husband Keith and I walked to the main entrance to find a cab, the rain turned into a torrential downpour. We had no umbrellas so I hid my camera under my trench coat. The driver dropped us off at the Burgermeister's office, a small unassuming, three-level, cream-colored stucco-looking building with a high-pitched, gabled, corrugated roof. Keith and I rushed to the door, pulling our coats over our heads.

As hard as I pulled on the big metal doorknob of the city administration building, the door wouldn't budge. Through the pouring rain I saw a sign stating that office hours were eight in the morning until noon, Monday through Friday. We had missed office hours by less than one minute! Keith and I stood there dumbfounded, when suddenly the door opened. As the person exited, my husband quickly dashed inside and I followed close behind.

Beyond the counter in the entryway, a woman was putting on her coat. Drenching wet with plastered hair and black mascara running down my face, I pleaded with her to help me, explaining I had come all the way from America to get some records and hadn't known the office hours. I was relieved when she gave me a sympathetic look and asked to see my passport, then she turned to a large, dusty leather-bound book.

Within two minutes she showed me my birth registration.

My date of birth was almost identical to what my mother had stated. The "Name of Father" line had been left blank.

After making several copies for me, she directed us upstairs for information about the DP camp.

The woman upstairs looked at me disapprovingly, curtly stating that they didn't have any records or pictures of the DP camp, but gave us a map of Altenstadt, pointing out the location of the camp. Map in hand, Keith and I took another taxi to the former DP barracks.

I leaned over the front seat, pointing to the location of the Wehrmacht. The driver was perplexed and asked, "Wehrmacht?"

I nodded.

The Wehrmacht Command Center in Altenstadt, used to house DPs after WW II, is once again a Germany military installation.

He shook his head, explaining that, once we arrived we would not be allowed beyond the gate. I pointed to my camera and told him I just wanted to take pictures of the place of my birth. Puzzled, the amused young man smiled, threw up his hands, and said, "Okay."

The rain had stopped by now, so when we got to the Wehrmacht, I jumped out and began taking pictures. In seconds, an armed officer bolted out of the Wehrmacht Command Center shouting, "Halt" and, with that guttural voice, transported me momentarily to the night when Jozef Walczek heard the same command, right before he was shot.

The guard cooled off when I showed him the birth registration I'd just obtained from the city offices. "I wish to take a picture of my birthplace," I told him.

Without a smile, but not quite as stern as before, the guard allowed me to finish my task, making it clear by holding out the outstretched fingers on his hand that I could only take pictures for five more minutes and that I was not to go beyond the barricade.

I never got inside, but a friend now living in Poland did succeed in entering the Wehrmacht facility. Her brother, who accompanied her on the trip, spoke fluent German and befriended the guard. She sent me a leaflet and picture of the Altenstadt plaque, which hangs in the Wehrmacht Museum. The plaque describes life in Altenstadt during the American occupation, stating that the mayor was ordered to clean the camp latrines and report daily at 8:00 a.m. to respond to requests from the UNRRA officials. Insight into camp life and the German peoples' disdain for the refugees is clearly illustrated in the following excerpt:

> The Poles really loved children! Between the Fall of 1946 and the Spring of 1952, 789 Polish children were born here in the main camp. They weren't that keen on respecting other peoples' property. For this reason the village had to introduce a local night watch. The watch was held from 11:00 p.m. until 4:00 a.m.

> After the Fall of 1948 it wasn't that pressing anymore to keep a watch over the fields because the season had advanced and the potatoes had been harvested. During the first quarter of 1949 the complaints accumulated about break-ins by members of the Polish camp [DP camp]. This was why the local night watch was introduced. It was only after the Poles were gone that the daily night watch could be dissolved.

As I looked beyond the Wehrmacht command center into the empty dry field behind, I thought of Stanislaw Sadovski losing his legs, Jozef Walczek losing his life, and Julie Walczek with the bright blue eyes. I pictured the heartbreak on my mother's face as she watched Jozef with his new family.

Before we left Germany, my husband and I stopped in Munich in search of DP records. A young man poured through large dusty volumes of books filed in the back office. He found no listing for Jozef Kurek but gave us an address in Berlin to investigate.

Visiting Altenstadt brought me no closer to meeting my father, but I felt grateful that I had been able to verify my birth date and time. That significant mystery was solved! The birth registration for Krys indicated that she was born at 10:40 a.m. and I was born at 11:55 p.m. on the exact same date, two years apart. The one-hour difference in the times was close enough to what Mom had claimed about our births, that one was born at noon and the other at midnight.

My birth registration also clarified that my birth records listed Paul Venckus as my father. Another handwritten note on the left side of the paper stated that Paul had given me his name, just as he had done for my sister Krystyna.

It was a surreal experience, to visit the historic places where my mother and father once lived, and to walk in their footsteps. I still wished I could ask Jozef, how could he abandon us like that? Why was he so angry all the time? He had the example of plenty of other survivors of the war, who were determined to make the most of the lives they had left. Why did Jozef Kurek choose to stay drunk and play cards instead of attending the DP University to prepare for a better life? Did he ever think of the consequences of his choices? Would he have stayed with Mother if Jozef Walczek hadn't died? Or would he have found some other excuse to leave us? I looked at the stars of the night sky, wondering if someday I would get my answers.

SEVEN

The Lake

Summer 1949: Rosenheim, Germany

With each passing day, my mother's sense of doom and fear of the unknown grew. She could see no way through the dark feeling of foreboding that she'd been living under after Jozef had abandoned us in a squalid displaced persons camp. Several times a day, she walked around a nearby lake with my sister and me to clear her mind. Krys was three and I was one at the time. Terrified she would be ordered to return to war-ravaged, communist-occupied Poland, she'd begun to feel any future happiness was slipping away. She began to think about ending our lives.

The first time I heard my mother tell me this dark secret, we were sitting at her kitchen table and I had asked her what happened after Jozef abandoned us. She sat in silence for a long time, and then said, "I met Paul and we came to America."

I knew the story couldn't be that simple. The love of her life had just left her with two small children, taking with him her dream of coming to America. I pressed harder.

"We were living at the Rosenheim Displaced Persons Camp. Jozef was in Bernau-Chiemsee. When the UNRRA agreed to transfer me from Altenstadt to Rosenheim to be closer to Bernau-Chiemsee, just sixteen miles away, I grabbed onto the idea that Jozef and I would reunite. Once our family was together again, we could fulfill my childhood dream of immigrating to America."

"You could forgive him after the way he treated you?"

"I loved Jozef. I would forgive him."

I slowly shook my head.

"My friends encouraged me to forget Jozef and make a new life. I tried. But my options became more limited with each passing month and the threat of deportation to Poland started to appear inevitable. I knew if I went back to Poland, the Communists would take you and Krys away from me, and I would be sent to Siberia or placed into hard labor."

Immigrating to America as a single mother was not possible. Women in this situation had to choose between freedom and their children. The idea of giving up children for adoption to begin a new life for themselves appeared to be a good solution. Not easy, but better than the alternatives.

People throughout Europe and America were eager to adopt the thousands of babies born in the DP camps. The UNRRA staff, as well as Mother's friends, persuaded her to place Krys and me with a family for adoption. For as long as she could hold out, Mother adamantly refused, but the pressure intensified. She was ridiculed for having nothing to offer her daughters. One of her friends called her "stupid" for not surrendering her children to have a better life for themselves. Her friends were sincere, the situation was dire, and the temptation was great. Mother began to feel guilty for depriving Krys and me of a better life. That feeling gnawed at her, and the next time a prospective family visited the camp, she agreed to meet with them.

My mother's face was wistful and sad as she talked about that critical moment.

With a sense of sadness, Mom told me, "The faces of those prospective adoptive parents lit up when they saw Krys and you. They couldn't stop talking about how beautiful the two of you were. They promised to give you the best of care. They described their comfortable home and life in Russia."

"What kind of people were they?" I asked.

"They said they were both university professors. They vowed to give you an extraordinarily good life. They would buy you pretty clothes, feed you very well, take you on trips around the world, and provide a good education. I was overwhelmed with gratitude for their genuine enthusiasm and their promise of an extraordinarily good life for you and Krys. I wanted you and your sister to have a good life, knowing I couldn't give that to you, so I agreed to the adoption.

"During the next several weeks, while I waited for the adoption papers to be processed, I couldn't eat or sleep. The thought of losing Krys and you consumed every moment of my days and nights. You were the only joy in my life! I couldn't bear the thought of life without my babies, yet the thought of depriving you of a better life tore at my soul.

"The day of surrendering you to the Russian couple came much too quickly. I could barely breathe when I heard the knock on the door. I tried to compose myself, but my knees were so weak I shook as I was walking to the door.

"The beaming faces of the happy couple did nothing to ease my agony that the moment had come. Quietly, I picked you up and held you in my arms. I took Krys's hand and kissed both of you, to say goodbye. The couple spoke softly, trying to coax you from my arms, but you tightened your grip around my neck each time they came close.

"I started to sob uncontrollably. I couldn't give you up! I looked at the husband and wife and told them, with all the strength of my being, "I can't and I won't give up my children." Stunned, they walked out the door without saying another word."

As soon as Mother made the decision not to give us up for adoption, the thought of receiving a Notice of Deportation to Poland obsessed her. Any hope of a new life elsewhere seemed undeniably out of reach. She could not envision any future happiness and she began to think that the way out was to end our lives.

"One day, the lake seemed to be pulling at my very soul. I stared trancelike into the water. How easy it would be to walk into its depths, holding us tight as the three of us became submerged. Any fears I had of never seeing you again would end.

"As we stood at the edge of the lake, Krys, a precocious three-year-old, pleaded, 'Mama, what are we doing here? Let's go home. I'm hungry!' But her voice seemed far away and I was oblivious to everything and everyone, except the beckoning water.

"Suddenly, I felt a hand gently touching my shoulder. I turned, but no one was there. I heard Krys's voice pleading with me to take us home, bringing me back to reality. I felt a surge of strength and determination. I vowed to survive whatever came our way. I had already survived this far. I took Krys by the hand, carried you in my arms, turned my back on the lake, and headed toward the camp."

The day that my mother decided not to end our lives, she discovered transfer orders in her mail slot. Her hands were shaking and she could barely open the piece of paper that read: "Notice of Transfer to Mittenwald."

Krystyna and Maria, Rosenheim Lake, Germany, 1949.

Nestled in the foothills of the Swiss Alps, Mittenwald was the nearest DP camp to Garmisch, ten miles from where Jozef had been transferred.

Many more restless nights were spent conflicted over which direction my mother should take in her life. She passed those sleepless nights cleaning the entrance steps to the former residence of the SS, now a newly converted DP barracks.

"I saw Jozef several times in Garmisch. With each visit, any illusions I had about a future with him had to be let go, but I couldn't get him out of my mind. I didn't want to let him go, because he is the father of my children and for that I will always love him."

I watched Mom's face turn sad in the dusky light as the night sky turned from gold to pink then black.

E I G H T

America

Autumn 1949: Mittenwald, Germany

One night in Mittenwald, a man with dark brown hair and cornflower blue eyes stopped to talk to Mother as she was cleaning the stairs. Pausing at the foot of the stairs, the man remarked, "Many people live in these barracks, but I only see you cleaning them."

Deep in her own thoughts, she barely looked up. "I don't mind cleaning. It gives me something to do late at night."

The man gave her an apple and orange, thanked her for her work, and walked up the stairs to his room.

He stopped by again one night and, finding my mother cleaning the steps, asked if she had family at the Mittenwald camp. Mother told me that she couldn't bear to speak of Jozef to the man, but described her two young daughters to him. She told him that the little girls' father had died.

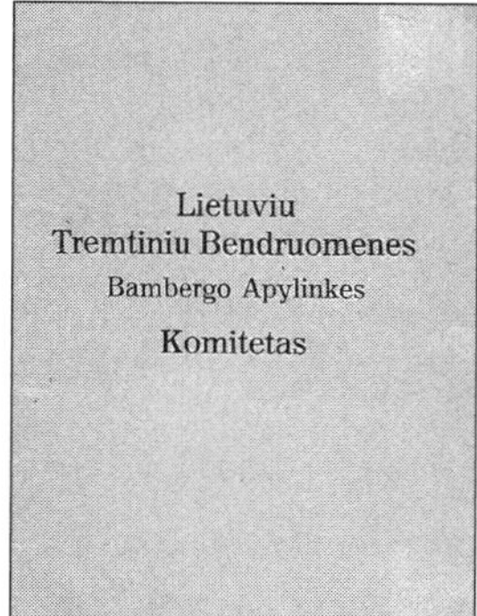

Lietuviu
Tremtiniu Bendruomenes
Bambergo Apylinkes
Komitetas

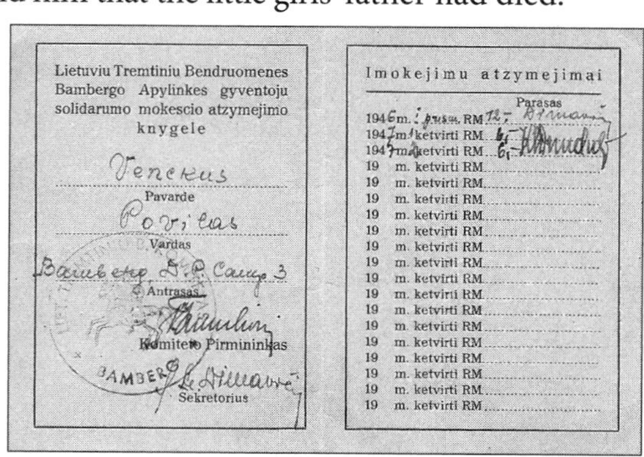

Lietuviu Tremtiniu Bendruomenes
Bambergo Apylinkes gyventoju
solidarumo mokescio atzymejimo
knygele

Venckus
Pavarde

Povilas
Vardas

Bamberg D.P. Camp 3
Antrasas

Komiteto Pirmininkas

Sekretorius

Imokejimu atzymejimai

	Parasas
1946 m. ... RM ...	
1947 m. ketvirti RM ...	
1947 m. ketvirti RM ...	
19 m. ketvirti RM ...	
19 m. ketvirti RM ...	
19 m. ketvirti RM ...	
19 m. ketvirti RM ...	
19 m. ketvirti RM ...	
19 m. ketvirti RM ...	
19 m. ketvirti RM ...	
19 m. ketvirti RM ...	
19 m. ketvirti RM ...	
19 m. ketvirti RM ...	
19 m. ketvirti RM ...	
19 m. ketvirti RM ...	
19 m. ketvirti RM ...	
19 m. ketvirti RM ...	
19 m. ketvirti RM ...	
19 m. ketvirti RM ...	
19 m. ketvirti RM ...	
19 m. ketvirti RM ...	

Left: Displaced Persons Identification Card of Paul Venckus (front cover). Right: Record of Paul Venckus' camp transfers as a displaced person in Germany (inside of DP Identification Card)

In exchange for cleaning his room and washing and mending his clothes, the man began bringing Mother fresh oranges, apples, and meat daily. He brought her bread with lard and bacon bits and offered his food ration stamps to her. They spoke German to each other, the common language for most displaced persons. The man's name was Povilas (Paul) Venckus.

Paul worked long hours for a U.S. engineering company under contract to help rebuild Germany, receiving good wages and food rations. He was working on building a chapel in the foothills of Luttensee Mountain in Mittenwald.

A priest often accompanied Paul to his chapel worksite and the two of them talked about the future. Paul told the priest, "If I find the right woman, I'll marry her in this chapel."

Paul was born in 1904, in the small Lithuanian village of Girdvainiai Kreis Telsiai. From one of the wealthiest families in the area, his parents owned a substantial amount of acreage and a large house. His parents had died when Paul was a young boy, and his uncle took ownership of the home and property and raised him. Paul told the priest that his uncle was a brutal man and beat him severely. He developed a stutter whenever subjected to significant stress.

Reminiscing about his homeland, Paul proudly told the priest, "When my uncle passed away, I reclaimed the house and the farm. On my own, I worked the farm hard and maintained the buildings and the land impeccably: no chips, cracks, or faded paint. My place had the reputation of being the best in the area. I owned and rented out the only thrashing machine in the region."

Paul's business acumen led to him becoming very successful and affluent. Paul married and he and his wife had five children. He left the farm in 1940 to defend Lithuania against the Russian invasion.

"While I was in service, my pregnant wife went into labor and died giving birth when her appendix ruptured and the Russian officials occu-

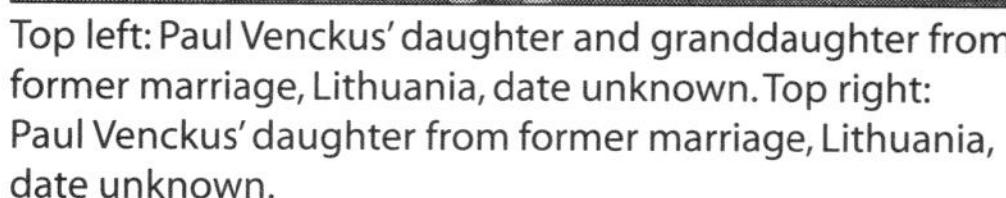

Top left: Paul Venckus' daughter and granddaughter from former marriage, Lithuania, date unknown. Top right: Paul Venckus' daughter from former marriage, Lithuania, date unknown.
Above: First Communion celebration of Paul's granddaughter, Lithuania, date unknown. Right: Paul's son, Ignas, poses in front of family house in Girdvainiai Kreis Telsiai, Lithuania, 1938.

pying Lithuania refused to allow her medical care. Two of my five children also died during the war. The Soviets confiscated my property and I no longer had a place of my own. My remaining three children had been taken and scattered throughout Europe. I searched frantically for them, I always will."

As Paul worked toward building a new future for himself and for Germany, his friendship with Mother gradually grew into feelings of love, but he was initially reluctant to start a new life with a woman who had two very young children. After many months of being with her, he became captivated by her energy and happiness. He observed that she worked hard and took exceptional care of Krys and me. He decided Mother was the woman with whom he wanted to rebuild his life. Paul asked the priest if he thought she would marry him.

The priest laughed and said, "You should be asking her, not me!"

That same priest and Mother had many conversations. She was candid with him. My mother told me that she said to the priest, truthfully, "I would only marry Paul to help me and my children get to America. I still care deeply for Jozef."

Chapel in the foothills of Luttensee Mountain in Mittenwald, Germany, where my mother and stepfather Paul were married.

The priest assured her, "Paul will provide you a good life. His honesty, good character, and strong work ethic might eventually outweigh these feelings you have toward Jozef. In time, you may come to love Paul."

My father and mother married in May of 1950, in the chapel that he had helped construct on Luttensee Mountain, where the white, star-shaped edelweiss and brilliant yellow wildflowers covered the gentle slope. Their friends served cold cuts, bread, and pickles at the wedding reception.

Mom told me, "Most of the women in Mittenwald camp were envious. I overheard many conversations speculating how an 'ugly' woman like me could have caught such a good man!"

Within a few weeks of their marriage, Paul and Mother applied for immigration to the United States through Catholic Charities. The IRO advised them to amend the birth registrations for Krys and me, indicating Povilas Venckus as our father.

Mother received the amended birth certificates from Altenstadt and Pfaffenhofen in July 1950. On December 13, 1950, the Area Legal Officer of IRO Area 7 in Munich placed his official seal on the birth certificates listing Paul Venckus as the father. The documents were signed in Grafenaschau, a few miles from Garmisch, the last place Mother had seen Jozef.

I asked Mom, "Did Jozef have to agree to list Paul as our father?"

She said, "No, he didn't find out about my marriage until a friend of ours told him."

"What was his reaction?" I asked.

"Our friend said Jozef wished me well, that I deserved to have a good life."

As I thought about Mother's version of the story, I had my own ideas. I thought that the IRO would have required Jozef's presence at the legal proceedings. Mom had always stated that Grafenashau was the last place she saw Jozef, and Grafenashau is the place identified in the official seal of the IRO. He must have been present at the proceedings, and would have said those words to her directly.

I hope he did. I wanted the last words that Jozef spoke to my mother to be kind and gentle, like the time he told her he would always remember her. I wanted her to feel loved in the last words my father ever said to her.

For myself, I hoped that my father would have regretted giving us up, or at least thought twice about it.

• • •

Resettlement teams screened and interrogated all refugees seeking immigration. The United States established a twenty-two-step process of checking the viability of each candidate, including their medical records and employment skills, an FBI investigation, and a records check of the Nazis' Berlin Document Center. The voluminous paperwork, measuring seventeen yards by some accounts, took three to twelve months to process.

After waiting almost a year, the United States informed Paul and my mother that their application had been approved, and our family would be transferred to Bremerhaven, Germany, the port designated for immigration to America.

Bremerhaven Port, Germany, 1951.

I was too young for these memories to imprint, but I know them by heart from the stories my mother told me. I know that we took a train from Mittenwald to Bremerhaven, a 580-mile, seven-hour journey, and then stayed in Bremerhaven for two days for a final medical examination and security screening.

My research into the larger transit stories of history taught me that scheduling the orderly departure of hundreds of thousands of displaced persons, even with approved applications, required extraordinary organizational skills. The average shipload contained twelve hundred passengers, with one ship departing every two to three days.

Our family was scheduled to leave for America on the U.S. Naval ship *General S.D. Sturgis,* the first ship assigned to transport displaced persons to their new countries.

USNS *General S.D. Sturgis* commissioned to transport Germany's refugees to America, 1951.

Boarding that ship, Mother knew she would be leaving her homeland forever, in trade for a new life in America. A crewmember on one of the voyages wrote, "As we moved up the Weser River towards the sea, the passengers gradually fell silent. They realized they were leaving their mother continent, probably never to return again. As long as land was in sight, the DPs stood on deck, watching their pasts fade into oblivion ..."

I thought about those words, reflecting on Jozef and my thus far unsuccessful search to find him. I began feeling that he too had faded into oblivion, somewhere in that night sky, beyond my reach.

My mother and I talked about this journey and I tried to picture myself as a small child on board this ship, headed for a country on the other side of the ocean.

Mom told me, "The voyage took ten days, but to me it seemed interminable. The ship was extremely congested and our living conditions were difficult. We were all seasick. The four of us made the voyage in steerage, a great big area in the bottom of the ship with bunk beds and hammocks. The men and the women were separated: women worked in the kitchen; men cleaned the decks, lavatories, and eating areas. Everyone ate at standup tables, except for mothers with small children; we were given access to a dining room formerly used by the ship's officers.

"A perpetual stench permeated the ship. One day, Krys could no longer stand the horrible smell of people getting sick, and she snuck out of steerage and crept up to the top deck. She found a spot by the rail, next to a large pole. Krys told me in later years, because she does remember some parts of the trip, that to her the ship appeared to be at a standstill, swaying back and forth but going nowhere. All she saw was endless water, no land, and she feared the ocean would surround her for the rest of her life!"

"How did it feel to finally reach land?" I asked.

"When the immigrants finally spotted the Statue of Liberty, most of us cried. I was no exception. The ship docked at Ellis Island and we stood in line with the twelve hundred other passengers, waiting impatiently to touch the soil of America.

"Upon arrival, we were subjected to the same approval

Left: Ellis Island, New York, 1951.
Below: Passenger manifest, USNS *General S.D. Sturgis,* August 1951.

Form I-415
TREASURY DEPARTMENT
United States Customs Service
UNITED STATES DEPARTMENT OF JUSTICE
Immigration and Naturalization Service
(Rev. 1-3-48)

Form approved.
Budget Bureau No. 43-R019-3.

MANIFEST NO. 34

MANIFEST OF IN-BOUND PASSENGERS (ALIENS)

Class DP from Bremerhaven (Port of embarkation), 7th Aug, 19 51

on USNS "GENERAL S.D. STURGIS" (Name of vessel) arriving at port of New York, N.Y. AUG 17 1951, 19 51

LINE No.	(1) FAMILY NAME—GIVEN NAME / DESTINATION IN UNITED STATES	AGE (Years)	SEX (F—M)	(2) MARRIED OR SINGLE	(3) TRAVEL DOC. NO. / NATIONALITY	(4) NUMBER AND DESCRIPTION OF PIECES OF BAGGAGE	(5) HEAD TAX COLLECTED	(6) THIS COLUMN FOR USE OF MASTER, SURGEON, AND U. S. OFFICERS
1	VAIKUTIS Hubertus 149 Madison Ave. New York, N.Y.	39.	Ma	S	I-1383960 Lithuanian	37	No	
2	VELVERSKY Jaroslav Kertel's Ranch, Guerneville, California	36	Ma	Md	I-1265155 Czech		No	
3	V[illegible] Povilas 107 E. Portage, Sault St.,Marie Mich.	46	Ma	Md	I-418504 Lithuanian		No	
4	V[illegible] Julia 107 E. Portage St. Marie, Mich.	32	F	Md	I-418505 Polish		No	
5	V[illegible] Krystyna 107 E. Portage, Sault St. Marie Mich.	5	F	S	I-418506 Polish		No	
6	V[illegible] Maria 107 E. Portage, Sault St. Marie, Mich.	3	F	S	I-418507 Polish		No	
7	VERMANIS Janis 3723 Washington Ave.,Cincinnati, Ohio	27	Ma	S	I-1383632 Latvian		No	
8	VIDA Mihaly. 218 N. 5th St. Indianna Pa.	41	Ma	Md	I-518217 Stateless		No	
9	VIDA Elizabet 218 N. 5th St. Indianan Pa.	36	F	Md	I-518216 Stateless		No	
10	VIDA Mihaly 218 N. 5th St. Indiana Pa.	12	Ma	S	I-518338 Stateless		No	

process that had been in place for decades. Doctors observed us as we ascended the stairs, looking for any signs of physical difficulty. A cursory physical exam to detect any obvious health problems was next."

My research described how symbols were drawn in chalk on the clothing of ill patients, indicating potential health problems. Two percent of those applying for admission into the United States were sent back on the basis of chronic disease or criminal activity. After the physical exam, the Immigration and Naturalization Service (INS) asked the immigrants twenty-nine questions regarding their backgrounds. The whole procedure lasted around five hours.

Mom said, "We spent the first night in the U.S. on Ellis Island, in one huge room furnished with row upon row of bunker beds with cots. The next morning the INS informed us that we would not be going to St. Marie, Michigan, as the Passenger Manifest indicated, but to Denver, Colorado. This excited me. I had heard of the Rocky Mountains and envisioned my new home to be much like Husne.

"We remained on Ellis Island for two days, and then took a bus to the train station, where we boarded for Chicago, and our final destination, Denver. The countryside from New York to Chicago was green until we headed west towards Denver, crossing through Nebraska, when the landscape turned brown. I gazed out the windows during the long journey and found myself feeling disappointed by the dry, brittle grasses and tumbleweed. This was hardly the picturesque countryside of my homeland. I expected a land of riches and streets paved in gold. It was hard to conceal my disillusionment and discontent. Here I was, starting a new life with a man I hardly knew, a man who made me and my children feel safe and who had given us the gift of America. But he was a man I did not love. Each time I looked at Paul, I tried not to think about Jozef. No matter what I did or where I was, I could not stop loving Jozef."

• • •

Catholic Charities had sponsored our immigration to America. A childless, middle-aged couple, Nellie and Ed, had agreed to provide us with housing and a job on a farm. Nellie, a trim, neatly dressed woman with short, graying hair styled in waves, greeted Krys and I coolly the first time we met and gave us a brown tabby kitten as a gift, without making a warm production out of it. I held the furry bundle up to my face, nuzzling it on my cheek, thanking her, but Nellie frowned.

We rarely saw Nellie after that first greeting, but Ed spent most of his day on the farm so we saw him frequently. When Krys and I felt carefree and childlike, giggling and chasing each other around our shack, Ed became irritated, gruffly demanding, "Be quiet and stop running around!" One day a gigantic bumblebee made its way into our shack. The angry buzzing and swarming terrified Krys and I and we screamed hysterically. Ed burst through the door with a sharp admonition, and we soon learned to keep our voices down in his presence.

Most of the time, Ed and Nellie kept their distance from us, although their house was less than one-hundred-fifty feet from our shack. Eventually they warmed up to us, however, and Nellie decided to teach English to Mom, Krys, and me; Dad had no spare time.

Nellie made Krys and me stand at attention while we repeated each letter: "A" "B" "C" … We had to repeat the sounds until they were pronounced perfectly, enunciating each letter clearly. She rarely praised us; we knew our pronunciation had satisfied her when she allowed us to go to the next letter. After we had memorized the entire alphabet, Nellie began teaching us numbers.

By the time Krys started first grade, she could understand and speak English. Krys walked two miles to the one-room schoolhouse, crossing farmland and a canal to get there. The teacher wanted to give her a warm welcome and asked her questions to put her at ease. Krys gave her name and the teacher wrote it on the blackboard, but Krys couldn't read and thought the teacher had scribbled. The teacher asked Krys where she was from, and she answered "Germany." A few students gasped. Krys was mortified when she heard one of the students whisper, "She's a Nazi!"

Two years after our arrival, Ed became terminally ill and the farm was sold. Catholic Charities transferred us to a small five-acre farm in Wheat Ridge, a suburb of Denver, where Dad went to work for Mount Olivet Cemetery, making cement vaults for caskets. This time, instead of just the washtub being filled with our worldly possessions, the entire trunk of Father Kolka's car contained our household goods.

My stepfather was a quiet, unassuming man, who worked from dawn to dusk. His day started at 4:30 each morning. I never heard him stirring downstairs—he would just quietly close the door and go out to work on our small five-acre farm in Wheat Ridge. Catholic Charities allowed us to rent the place for twenty-five dollars a month in exchange for Dad working as the gatekeeper to the cemetery. He plowed, irrigated, and hoed the farmland for hours before returning for Mother's coffee and breakfast.

Krys started third grade in a new school. It was a large, two-story red brick building with a huge oak at the main entrance. The school had been recently expanded to accommodate the population explosion from the baby boomers. This time Krys told her teacher and classmates she was from Rochester, a place she found on a map of New York. When I started school, I was fluent in German, Polish, and English. The teachers thought I had a speech impediment and sent me to speech therapy to learn to speak English without a German and Polish accent.

We didn't have a car so Mom, Krys, and I walked a mile to the local AG grocery store, a two-aisle, four-hundred-square-foot building whose floorboards creaked with each step. We carried paper bags full of groceries, Mom giving the lightest bag, filled with bread, to me. We took the bus to church, walking a mile uphill from the stop. Mom made us wear jeans underneath our dresses on cold, snowy days. We found a recessed corner to remove them before entering the church. Shopping malls did not exist in 1950s Denver, so we took the bus downtown for major purchases, usually only at Easter and Christmastime.

Mom began working as a nurse's aide in one of the suburban hospitals, and with the additional income bought a car, a 1951 Hudson Spitfire for three hundred dollars. Krys and I contributed to household expenses by collecting pop bottles tossed from cars, redeeming them for two cents each, and selling fresh sweet corn from the trunk of our car. With any extra money, we bought school supplies and paid for movies and the amusement park. Mom purchased an old pedal-driven Singer sewing machine, transforming the colorful grain sacks she used for feeding the calf into clothes for Krys and me.

Our new house had indoor plumbing, a large pot-bellied stove in the massive kitchen, and electricity. We did not have central heating, but between the radiator in the living room and the pot-bellied stove, we stayed warm. Krys and I slept in the loft upstairs, touching our hands on the chimney to stay warm while getting dressed for school.

Dad and Mom both had good jobs now and we lived in a decent, safe house, had plenty of food, and enough money to go out to dinner once every three months. Krys and I attended excellent public schools, participated in sports, and I joined the local Girl Scout Troop. Eventually we bought a TV set; it was in an upright wooden cabinet, the back end full of large glass tubes. We got snowflakes quite often on the screen, but Dad didn't mind until the picture started to roll. The snowflakes didn't bother him, he could still make out shadowy figures, but the rolling irritated him, and he would start fidgeting with the controls until it stopped. We got a party-line telephone, two rings signaling our number. Now we felt we were truly rich and had fully assimilated into the American way of life.

Mom, a vibrant, earthy woman, made friends easily. Our American neighbors warmly accepted us, intrigued by Mom's stories about the war. Dad and Mom joined the Polish Club of Denver to dance polkas, eat traditional Eastern European food, and speak their native language. Mom served Polish sausages, cheese, and coffee cake to the Fuller Brush man, and any other door-to-door salesman that came to our house selling pots and pans, in keeping with the old European hospitality tradition. We couldn't have been happier, living the American dream.

Each morning we awakened to the smell of bacon and Mom's voice coaxing us down to breakfast. Dad would have already eaten by then and gone to work at his full-time job. He'd come home for lunch, which Mom had prepared and ready for him. After work, he tended to the chickens, turkeys, steer, and the garden again. During the wintertime, he chopped wood for the pot-bellied stove that warmed our house.

I often went with Dad on his wood-chopping expeditions, helping him carry the wood to the trunk of his car. We seldom talked. I kept my distance from the deafening sound and smell of gasoline from the chainsaw. I would see him beyond the clump of dead trees, sawing and chopping, while I would be in my make-believe world of clearing dirt and rubble to make an imaginary castle. Once I overheard Dad telling Mom how well I had cleared out a large fallen tree and made an impeccably clean house out of it. I was so proud he noticed. When Catholic Charities forced us to move from our rented house at Mount Olivet, because the church needed the little farm to expand the cemetery, Dad made the down payment on our new house in Denver, which he and Mom bought by selling the neatly stacked firewood piles.

Over the next years, we assimilated into our new way of life, attending school and church functions and social events. Europe became a distant past as we became immersed in life in America. Mom learned to soften her pronunciation of "dis" and "dat" to "this" and "that," repeating the sounds until she mimicked the pronunciation of her American friends. Still, she missed her homeland and continued to attend the Polish Club.

Although Dad and I never had any deep conversations, he and I bonded and became very close. We understood each other at a basic level. He frequently told me I was "smart" and a "good businesswoman." Many times throughout my career in the Treasury Department and then the U.S. Department of Commerce, when I was having a bad day or felt I had done something stupid, I would remember Dad's encouraging words.

Dad loved Mom deeply even though he knew her heart wasn't his. He gave her his paycheck to use as she deemed necessary and seldom complained about her purchases. The few times they disagreed, Dad was the first to give in. Mom took exceptional care of Dad, fixing him home-cooked meals, washing, ironing, and mending his clothes, and tending to his needs. But she seldom showed any affection toward Dad, at least none that I witnessed.

A memory that is etched in my mind is of a time when Mom was out of town for over a week, attending Krys's daughter Michele's wedding. Mom prepared Dad's meals before she left and I stopped by daily to check in on him, now an aging grey-haired man.

Each day he asked me, "When is Momma coming home?"

When I picked Mom up at the airport and brought her to the house, Dad was waiting for her on the front porch, sitting in his rocking chair. He immediately rose to greet her with a big smile on his face, and went to embrace her, but she stiffened. I felt love and sympathy for Dad and after that I was more attentive toward him, trying to show him how grateful I am for all that he gave us.

When Mom came to America, she exchanged the ancient Carpathian Mountains for the Rockies' purple mountains and the only man she ever loved for a man she didn't love, even though he was decent, hard working, and loving. Eventually, Mom made peace with the past and the pain from the war and Jozef's abandonment had healed.

NINE

The Search for Jozef

Months turned into years, then decades, and I still had not found Jozef. As the mystery deepened, so did my fantasies of him being a daring, dashing pilot. The Blue Angels performed air shows in Denver for Memorial Day tributes; I watched the fighters soaring steeply into the blue sky, the jet stream leaving circular patterns as the pilots performed their acrobatics high above the city, the deafening sound of roaring engines diminishing when they became shiny, glittering diamonds in the endless sky. I thought about my favorite lines from "High Flight," a poem written by John Gillespie Magee Jr.:

> Oh! I have slipped the surly bonds of Earth
> And danced the skies on laughter-silvered wings …
> Up, up the long, delirious burning blue
> I've tipped the wind-swept heights with easy grace
> Where never lark, or ever eagle flew—…
> And … Put out my hand and touched the face of God.

If I found Jozef I would recite the entire poem to him and ask him what exhilarated him most about flying: Was it the forward thrust of the throttle that started the engine screaming as the plane shuddered out of the pull of gravity and soared into the vast freedom of the blue sky? Or was it the satisfaction of seeing his enemy, the destroyer of

Poland, spiral to earth, exploding into an inferno? His answer would give me a good glimpse into his character.

November 1980: Denver, Colorado

The wind howled as it whirled the leaves angrily in all directions. I buttoned the top of my coat and held the collar over my ears as I rushed up the sidewalk to Mother's house, being careful not to slip on the icy stairs. The next day was Thanksgiving, and I had promised her I would help prepare the lavish meal.

My mother was in an especially talkative mood, grateful that I had braved the brutal weather to help her in the kitchen. I could smell the sage and herbs in the turkey dressing she was stirring. She excitedly told me everything she was preparing for the dinner, asking my opinion about some of the dishes. She wanted to make sure everyone would have enough to eat and that they would like the food. Besides our immediate family, six other people were invited, and she told me she had bought a new dress to celebrate the day. She asked me what I was going to wear.

"I think I'll wear my brown wool skirt and yellow sweater—they're nice Thanksgiving colors. What do you think?"

"Yes, you look good in those colors. Come, let me show you my new dress."

We walked to her bedroom and she turned on the light in the walk-in closet, removing a beautiful, lavender silk-looking dress from the rack.

"Oh Mom, it's beautiful!" I felt the fabric and asked her what kind of material it was.

"I don't know. Your father would know—he came from Lublin, where they make the best and fanciest fabrics in the world."

I hoped my face didn't reveal too much excitement over the fact that she had just given me a major clue about Jozef Kurek, my father, for whom I was still searching.

The clue became one of many important pieces to the puzzle I was putting together, but instead of Jozef emerging as a valiant hero, the pieces were now showing Mom as an indomitable, resilient woman with quiet courage.

When I was about eight years old, Mom religiously watched *Queen for a Day* and would cry at the stories. A popular TV series in the 1950s, the show was similar to contemporary reality shows. *Queen for a Day* contestants were middle-aged and older women who appeared on the show and gave detailed accounts of the hardships and tragedies they had endured. The contestant with the most heartbreaking story was proclaimed Queen for a Day: a sparkling jeweled crown was placed atop her head, a red velvet mantel with white fur around her shoulders, and a dozen long-stemmed roses laid in her arms, as tears streamed down her face.

One time I was watching the show with my mother and she commented, "I should be a contestant, because I would be selected queen."

Mom was certain that she would win the grand prize. "A book should be written about my life!"

At the time, I laughed; at age eight, I had no way of being able to understand the extent of her courage and strength in putting the pieces of her broken life back together again and again.

August 9, 1998: Golden, Colorado

The caterer busied himself setting up a large silver urn of coffee and went back and forth to the van, bringing in silver chafing dishes of food we had selected from the menu. My guests would be arriving in half an hour. Our first grandchild was due in October and I wanted to have an elaborate party to celebrate; Mother had asked me to invite her old friend, Janka Mucha.

Janka Mucha was coming to my house for the baby shower I was giving for my daughter-in-law and I had figured out how I would be able to have a private conversation with her. I had seen her on rare occasions in the last thirty-seven years since I first overheard her whispering with my mother about who my father really was. I was anxious to have a private talk with her; I had never dared to ask her questions about Jozef over all those decades.

Janka and her husband Antoni had lived in the Altenstadt DP camp with Jozef and Mother. Antoni and Jozef were good friends and frequently played cards together. When Jozef abandoned us, it was Janka and Antoni that looked after Mother, Krys, and me, giving us emotional support and extra food. Both Janka and Antoni confronted Jozef about his desertion, but to no avail. They had immigrated to Denver a few months before we had. I never asked Janka about Jozef before, because to have asked her in front of my mother would have been brazen and disrespectful.

Mom had told Janka about my new house and Janka wanted to see it. My house was far from being a mansion, but the kitchen itself was larger than the entire shack we had lived in upon our arrival in America. I was delighted that I would be seeing Janka today.

When she arrived with Mom, the caterer offered them champagne, and they sat on the couch sipping it. When the glass was emptied, I offered to take Janka on a grand tour. Mom was busy trying out the hors d'oeuvres.

I took Janka upstairs, starting the tour with one of the smaller bedrooms. When we got to the spacious master bedroom, she looked around and spotted a picture of me in my late twenties.

"You look so much like your father."

This was the opening I needed! "What can you tell me about him?"

"He was an elegant man; very handsome. All the women chased after him. It is sad what happened between Jozef and your mother, but everyone expected it. He could be wild sometimes."

"Do you know where he is?"

"Somewhere in Germany, if he's still alive."

I handed Janka a pen and some paper that I had deliberately placed on my dresser. "Would you write his name for me?"

Janka looked up at me somewhat perplexed and wrote his name. As incredulous as it may sound, I never knew the correct spelling of Jozef's surname until that moment.

Now that I had the correct spelling, I believed I would make better progress, as the letters I had previously sent to Germany always included an explanation that the spelling may be Kurick, Kurik, Kuric, or Kurak.

However, it turned out that using the correct spelling in my subsequent letters to Germany didn't produce any better results. Our family albums continued to be filled with pictures of the Sutton family celebrating baptisms, birthdays, graduations, and weddings.

I continued to wonder if Jozef was alive. Did he ever reflect on the family he had left behind? Perhaps grandchildren from his new family already surrounded him, while he told stories about the war.

I was beginning to think that Jozef would always remain beyond those stars of the night sky and I would never find him—until the miracle of the Internet came along.

I retrieved my dusty boxes of notes about Jozef and feverishly began Googling. When I keyed in "Kurek" I came across a genealogical tree for the ancestors and descendants of the Pirowski family, which listed a Jozef Kurek who had been born in 1913 and whose mother's name was Victoria. The date of birth and his mother's name was a close match. This Jozef had a son, Piotr, born in 1948. It could have been possible for Jozef to have fathered this child.

My heart started beating faster; this was my strongest lead to date. I tracked down the webmaster, Artur. He was interested in helping me, and after obtaining permission from Piotr, gave me his email address. Piotr confirmed his father had been a Polish officer and had served in the Underground Army, but that it would not be possible for him to be my father because he had never been to Germany. I didn't accept Piotr's explanation. The pieces of the puzzle were all starting to come together—if he were in the Underground Army, he could have been in Germany.

I began researching the Jozef Kurek born in 1913: He was a Captain and recipient of Poland's highest military award, The Order of the White Eagle. This is what I had dreamed my father would be—a brave, fearless man—a hero! Maybe Mother had fabricated the story of Jozef in the DP camps to protect him. My imagination ran wild—I desperately wanted to believe this was my father, dismissing all inconsistencies in timelines and places.

Captain Jozef Kurek, Warsaw, Poland.

I continued corresponding with Piotr, convinced I had found my father. Piotr kept insisting it could not be possible, stating his father had never been in Germany during WWII as well as after 1945, giving this timeline:

- Up to 1945 he served in the Polish Underground Army in the Jedrzejow-Kielce region
- In June 1945 he married Piotr's mother
- From 1945 to 1948 he attended Jagiellonian University to change his profession

Piotr offered to send his father's transcripts from Jagiellonian University as proof his father could not possibly be my father as well.

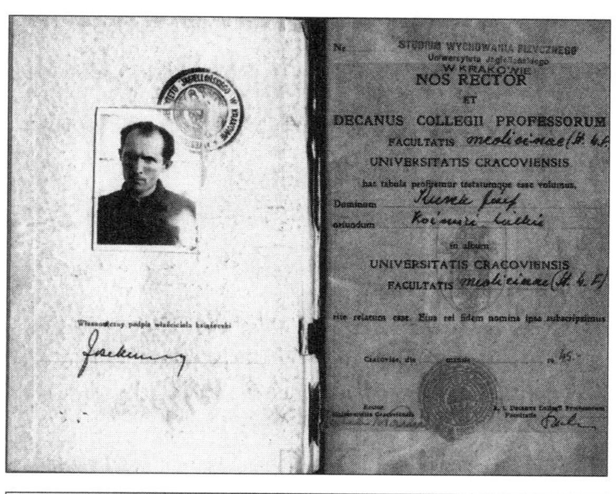

STUDIUM WYCHOWANIA FIZYCZNEGO
Uniwersytetu Jagiellońskiego
W KRAKOWIE

NOS RECTOR
ET
DECANUS COLLEGII PROFESSORUM
FACULTATIS *medicinae (St. W. F.)*
UNIVERSITATIS CRACOVIENSIS

Dominum *Kurek Józef*

UNIVERSITATIS CRACOVIENSIS
FACULTATIS *medicinae (St. W. F.)*

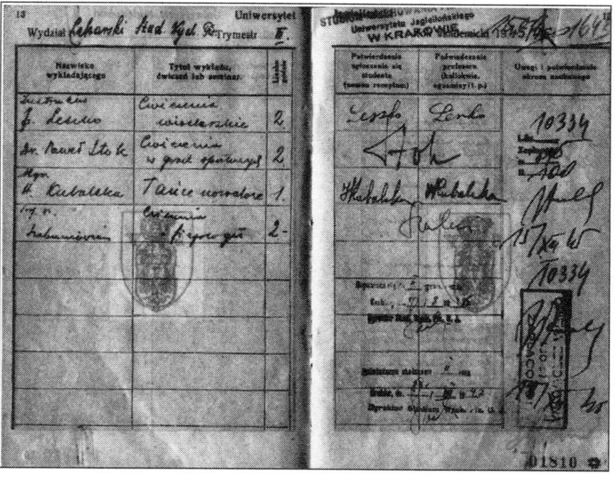

Uniwersytet
Wydział *Lekarski Stud. Wych. Fiz.* Trymestr

WKRAKOWIE

Nazwisko wykładającego	Tytuł wykładu, ćwiczeń lub seminar.	
J. Lesko	*Ćwiczenia*	*2*
Dr. Paweł Stock	*Ćwiczenia*	*2*
H. Kubalska	*Tańce*	*1*
	Ćwiczenia	*2*

01810

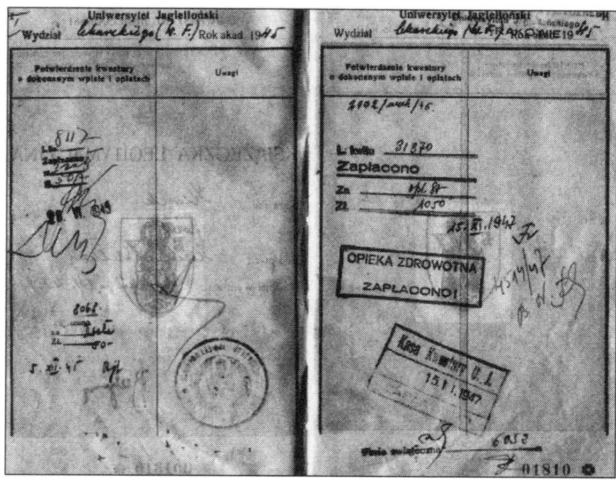

Uniwersytet Jagielloński
Wydział *Lekarskiego (St. W. F.)* Rok akad 19*45*

Potwierdzenie kwestury o dokonanym wpisie i opłatach	Uwagi

Uniwersytet Jagielloński
Wydział Rok akad 19

Potwierdzenie kwestury o dokonanym wpisie i opłatach	Uwagi

Zapłacono

OPIEKA ZDROWOTNA
ZAPŁACONO!

01810

Jagiellonian University transcript of Jozef Kurek, 1945–1948.

When I got the transcripts I scrutinized them for dates of attendance and any evidence of alteration, but there was none. I couldn't ignore the truth. Devastated, I sent an email to the webmaster of the Pirowski family tree website, Artur, to let him know Piotr and I were not related, and, if during his genealogical research he came across another Jozef Kurek with a similar background, I would sincerely appreciate him passing the information along to me. Artur and I corresponded for several months trying to solve the mystery of Jozef and why there were no records of my father in Poland or Germany. We speculated about him being an imposter, or a spy, and that many military records had been destroyed when Warsaw had been bombed to rubble. I began to feel Jozef would always be beyond my reach—beyond the stars of the night sky I had been gazing at for a lifetime. I gave up on the search, analyzing what to do next.

February 2002: Denver, Colorado

I was fifty-five years old and had been searching for Jozef for almost four decades. Mom was eighty-four and I had come to her house to help her bake cookies. She was rolling the dough for her Valentine's Day sugar cookies. I could smell the vanilla in the batch she had just made. She floured the large mound, and rubbed off the small scraps of dough from the rolling pin.

I watched the clock above the stove. When the buzzer went off, I grabbed two oven mitts, removed the large cookie sheets from the oven, and reached for the large bowl of red frosting.

I stopped to look out the window to see giant snowflakes falling.

I asked Mom if Valentine's Day was celebrated in Germany, and then, I'm not sure why, I blurted out, "What happened to my father anyway? Where is he?"

My mother looked angry. "Jozef is dead."

"When did he die?"

"I don't know. He's dead, so don't waste any more time thinking about him."

We finished making the cookies in silence.

When I got home I wrote a letter to Berlin requesting a death certificate for Jozef Kurek.

Four months later I received their response: they had no record of his death.

The next time I saw Mom, I informed her that Jozef wasn't dead. Her face turned white and she told me, "Yes, I lied to you, but it's for your own good."

"You really don't know what happened to him, do you?"

"You don't understand what living in a DP camp in Germany was like. We didn't sit around having fun. Our barracks were overcrowded and we felt the camp was one big warehouse where we were being stored until they found some other horrible place to put us. There was never enough food and people were tired of canned and boxed meat, vegetables, and potatoes. The DPs wanted to have normal food and a decent place to live."

Mom's face flushed as she remembered the hatred that displaced persons in Altenstadt felt toward the German people. "The disparity in housing and food supplies became more noticeable. While the German people had fresh food in plentiful supply, DPs lived in squalor. Basic necessities such as food, toiletries, clothing, and privacy were not available. Mothers made diapers for their babies by ripping their own clothes. As resentment built, the men began stealing supplies and food from nearby farms."

The UNRRA turned their heads and allowed the DPs to pilfer the farms. But the Germans protested, and the UNRRA had to put a stop to the practice. Warning notices were distributed to the DPs: Anyone caught raiding German farms would be arrested and imprisoned. The German people hated the DPs, and were angry that their soldiers and civilians were being jailed for war crimes while the UNRRA ignored the DPs offenses.

"Julie Walczek kept demanding that Jozef bring fresh food to her and her four children. Other men were stealing food for their families and she became angry and hostile toward Jozef for not doing the same. I heard that Jozef and some of his friends were raiding the nearby farms, and I begged him to stop, but he wouldn't listen to me. He wanted to make Julie Walczek happy."

My mother was talkative, seemingly anxious to free herself of holding the secrets of those times.

"Jozef was restless and began feeling oppressed by the endless days of having nothing meaningful to do. His new Julie kept pressuring him for meat to make pot roasts, pork chops, and gravy to pour over real potatoes. He and his card-playing friends stole vegetables from the gardens and livestock from the pastures, despite the UNRRA warning. One day Jozef and his friends found a pig that had wandered into a secluded area and they caught and killed it, then dragged it into the forest. They were in the middle of butchering it when the German police saw them and immediately arrested all four of them, taking them into town to be jailed. Jozef was not a good man. That's why I have not wanted you to find him."

I winced at the thought of Jozef being arrested, handcuffed, and imprisoned. I didn't like how the pieces of the puzzle were coming together. The idea that my father could be seen as a criminal appalled me.

As I integrated the distressing news, I began making excuses for him like Mom had. I convinced myself that stealing food was a justifiable action, considering the circumstances under which Jozef and the other DPs lived. But my sterling image of Jozef was tarnishing, and I realized that, if I ever did learn the entire truth, it might not match the fantasy I wanted to believe about him.

My mother was willing to disavow me of illusions now.

"Jozef wrote Julie Walczek many letters when he was in jail, but others told me that she wanted nothing to do with him. As a matter of fact, she moved in with Stanislaw Sadovski. Remember the man who lost his legs in a train accident? Thanks to settlement money from the tragedy, Sadovski offered Julie Walczek and her four daughters a good life.

"Jozef started writing letters to me, saying he had made the biggest mistake of his life. He told me that as soon as he was out of prison, we would be married and have a good life together."

I hung onto this idea. I fiercely wanted to believe that Jozef truly regretted leaving my mother, but I couldn't accept the notion that Jozef would suddenly become introspective in prison and realize he loved my mother. Julie Walczek had spurned Jozef, and he needed someone else to be there for him.

I didn't convey these thoughts to Mom, but while she was telling me this story I could tell that she was smart enough at the time not to believe him either. It must have been difficult for my mother to confront this remorseful Jozef, who now claimed he wanted to marry her. She had been through the emotional roller coaster with him so many times that she must have known she couldn't trust him.

"Time was running out for us—Jozef would not be released from prison until December 21, 1951, and if I waited for him we would miss the December 31 immigration deadline. Germany kept transferring Jozef from prison to prison as they were being rebuilt. The UNRRA transferred me every time Jozef was transferred, first to Rosenheim to be near him in Bernau-Chiemssee, then to Mittenwald when Jozef was in Garmisch. The UNRRA wanted to keep families together so we could immigrate or be repatriated as a unit."

"Where was the last time you saw Jozef?"

"Grafenaschau."

"What prison was he in?"

"Stottenheim, a jail about seventy miles from Stuttgart. But the jail burned down a long time ago, so they won't have any records of him."

That night, I took out my map of Germany and drew a circle approximating a seventy-mile radius around Stuttgart and began making a list of towns that sounded like "Stottenheim," pinpointing their locations. After staying up until three in the morning several times and still not finding the city, I gave up on that lead.

I focused on three key documents that I knew would provide the critical information I needed to trace Jozef:

- Military records from Poland
- Prisoner of War Certificate
- Arrest and imprisonment records

I hired a genealogist in Poland to visit Central Military Archives (Centralne Archiwum Wojskowe [CAW]) in Warsaw to make a list of every man named Jozef Kurek who had served during World War II. After receiving my notarized authorization, the genealogist spent several days at CAW and in a few weeks sent me a list of seventeen men, but none of them came close to the birth date of my father, which Mother had said was about 1915.

Next, I requested the Prisoner of War certificate from the International Red Cross in Geneva, Switzerland. They sent me a certificate for a Jozef Kurek born 1908 in Niemojew, Poland, and a letter stating he was the only person who could be my father. Although none of the information on the certificate matched what scant information I had, I pursued this lead for many months until it dead-ended. At one time, I was tracing four different men named Jozef Kurek, none of whom turned out to be my father.

I remembered the Stottenheim lead and found a German Justice Department website with an eighty-nine page list of German prisons. One was close to the phonetic spelling of Stottenheim—"Sachsenheim"—but I could find no address or telephone number. I wrote to the German

Justice Ministry and discovered the prison and all of its records had been destroyed in a fire. Mother had not lied to me about that.

I began sending out mass mailings to anyone named "Breitner." Das Telefonbuch (telephone directory) listed forty pages containing 389 Breitner names on their website, and I decided I would send out ten letters a day, hitting all of them in about a month. Das Telefonbuch recorded 607 people with the Kurek surname. I thought it odd that the Polish name had more listings than did the German one.

Keith never admonished me for staying up into the wee hours of the morning stuffing envelopes, and quite often helped me. None of the mass mailings resulted in finding Jozef, but I received many cards and letters from Germany, wishing me good luck.

My only hope of finding Jozef was through his arrest records. None of the logical places—Altenstadt, Munich, or Berlin—had a record of his arrest. The brick wall between that vital record and me wouldn't crumble. Although I had submitted a request to the International Tracing Service in Germany, I couldn't rely on them to find Jozef any time soon; I was one of the nine million applications they received for tracing services since the end of the war.

My only remaining source of information was my mother—the one person who didn't want me to find Jozef.

Mom was eighty-five years old by now and starting to have problems with her memory. She also had difficulties fixing meals and cleaning house. I hired home care to be with her through the day, and began seeing her every night to help her with dinner and bed. We made small talk, usually about Jozef, Wasyl, Dad, and her life in Ukraine and Germany.

Dad died in 1995 at the age of ninety. They had been married for forty-five years and Mom missed him. She frequently talked about what a good man he had been for bringing us to America.

During their long marriage, Mom rarely demonstrated affection toward Dad. Sometimes she seemed agitated by him, although she did not show hostility toward him. Now that he was gone, she said she felt lonely without him, and I could hear the warmth in her voice when she spoke of him.

I don't think Mom ever loved Dad in the same way she loved Jozef. The two men were complete opposites, in their physical appearance as well as their demeanor. Jozef was fiery and had the same adventurous spirit Mom possessed; Dad was temperate. After Dad's death, Mom came to appreciate the security he had given her, and thought fondly of him as a long-time friend and companion. That she never developed the passion for Dad that she had for Jozef was perhaps her only regret.

During one of my nightly visits to Mom, she seemed disturbed by a dream she had been having for the past several nights. In it, Jozef is standing at her front door, waiting to be let in the house. As she gets up, she sees Dad looking beseechingly at her. When she opens the door, Jozef smiles at her, tells her how sorry he is for having left her, and begs her to take him back.

"What do you say to Jozef?" I asked.

"I tell him I forgive him, and that I will take him back."

"What about Dad?"

After a long silence, Mom looks sad and replies, "It's just a dream."

Looking at my mother, I felt conflicted. Dad had been a loving husband to my mother and a decent, kind, hard-working father to me, but I, too, felt a great need and desire to see Jozef.

During the next few months, Mom seemed to be in a frenzied state of mind. Her memory was noticeably fading, yet, she clearly remembered people, places, and events that occurred sixty years ago. She couldn't remember what she had for lunch, or what day of the week it was, but she began reminiscing in detail about all the places she and Jozef had been together. There was a sense of urgency in her, as if she had to see Jozef before the end of her life. She may have thought now that Dad was gone, she had one last chance of fulfilling her hopes and dreams of being reunited with Jozef, or perhaps she had a desperate need for closure and peace before she died. Whatever her motives, she clearly wanted me to find Jozef—quickly.

One nondescript summer day, Mom and I were sitting in our favorite places on Mom's front porch having our usual conversation about Jozef and the war, and she told me he had been taken to Augsburg when he was arrested.

She had never mentioned Augsburg before, and I was skeptical. None of my inquiries to Germany had resulted in any information about Jozef. Nonetheless, when I got home I emailed the Augsburg Justice Department. Within a few days, I received a response. A Jozef Kurek, born May 4, 1916, in Grezowka, Poland, was in their archives!

I could barely type the word "Grezowka" into the Multimap.com website, my hands shook so much. My computer seemed to take forever to open the site when I hit the Enter key. Finally, after navigating the site, I found Grezowka was in the Lublin province, located near Lukow, a town known for its textile industry. Lublin, the year 1916, and the textile industry all matched the miniscule information Mom had given me about Jozef.

This Jozef Kurek had to be my father.

The Augsburg archivist stated that she would be unable to email the records to me, but would send them regular mail. Now that I had Jozef's date and place of birth, I sent a letter to the International Red Cross requesting his Prisoner of War certificate.

His rank was listed as "Schütze" which means "protection" in English. The thought of Jozef being a protected agent crossed my mind again.

Within a few weeks of receiving Jozef's POW certificate, I received his prison records; they matched. I anxiously scrutinized every word of his prison records.

Jozef's prison records indicated that he had been arrested June 12, 1949, indicted August 19, and imprisoned on August 26 in Garmisch.

COMITÉ INTERNATIONAL DE LA CROIX-ROUGE

DC/ARCH/EMU

Geneva, le 22.04.2004

ATTESTATION

The Cenral Tracing Agency has received the following information:

Name, first name	:	KUREK Jozef
Date of birth	:	04.05.1916
Place of birth	:	no information
Father's name	:	no information
Rank	:	"Schütze"
Incorporation	:	79 Inf. Regiment
Date of capture	:	04.10.1939 Deblin
Prisoner number	:	1997
Service number	:	no information
Place of internment	:	- present in Stalag VII-A on 28.10.1939 (according to a list dated 16.11.1939).
Liberation and repatration	:	no information
From	:	one list from German authorities.

Comité International de la Croix-Rouge
AGENCE CENTRALE DE RECHERCHES
GENEVE

My father's Prisoner of War certificate received from the International Red Cross in Geneva, Switzerland.

He transferred to Bernau-Chiemsee September 23 and returned to Garmisch September 29, 1949. It was the same summer in 1949 that my mother had contemplated ending our lives.

I carefully examined Jozef's prison records for his last place of residence. The Dachau refugee camp was listed. I sent a letter to the archivist at the Dachau Memorial Museum, which had previously been the location of the refugee camp after the war, requesting information on the Jozef Kurek born May 4, 1916, in Grezowka, Poland. They referred me to the Dachau city archives.

German law would not allow Dachau city officials to forward the data to me unless I could prove that I was a "closest" relative of his. I

Jozef's prison records from Augsburg, Germany, 1949.

emailed them the letter from the International Red Cross stating that only this "Jozef Kurek" could be my father, along with the POW certificate and my birth certificate from Altenstadt. My birth certificate did not list Jozef as my father, but I assured them that other German authorities had released Jozef's records to me.

The email from the Stadtarchiv Dachau stated: "Many thanks for forwarding the documents. Attached find a registration card with the mentioning of Josef Kurek. He died on January 10, 1976, in Dachau. We have no photograph of him here in the city archives, but you might contact his widow Helene Kurek."

I slumped in my chair, staring at the computer screen, unable to move. I re-read the email several more times and then bolted with the realization: I had found him—my search was over!

I downloaded Jozef's Residence Registration. He and Helene had lived in the same apartment since 1959.

I ran upstairs to my bedroom, where my husband lay sound asleep and shouted, "I've found him, I've found him!"

Keith woke up dazed. "What?"

I started talking a million words a second and jumping around the bed like a small child.

Keith could barely understand what I was saying, "It's him, it's him," I repeated until Keith was fully awake.

> I found Jozef at precisely 4:30 a.m. on July 2, 2004—nearly forty-three years from the time I first heard he was my father during that Fourth of July picnic in 1961 on Genesee Mountain, sponsored by the Polish Club of Denver.

The kindness of a stranger pouring over fifty-six-year-old handwritten records in the Augsburg archives finally solved the mystery.

Throughout my forty-three-year search, the number of strangers who wanted to help me find Jozef humbled me. Many people in Germany hand-carried my mass-mailings to anyone having the Kurek surname, house to house in their villages, asking for information. I had also emailed thousands of strangers in faraway lands and it was encouraging and heartwarming to receive responses from more than 90 percent of them.

My heart had sunk when I read that Jozef had died on January 10, 1976, but in a way I was prepared for it. I became elated to know that his widow was still alive. I could contact her and ask her questions about my father that had been burning inside me for years. I had no way of knowing my elation in finding Jozef would be followed by the most painful experience in my life, cutting deeply into my soul and testing my sense of self.

TEN

A Painful Truth

From the time I first began fantasizing about Jozef as a thirteen-year-old girl in 1961, it had never occurred to me that the real Jozef might disillusion me, and if it did, I pushed the thought away. Mother warned me he wasn't the person I imagined. I held close an image of a dashing Polish officer: entertaining, charming, a history aficionado and book enthusiast, meticulous about his appearance; successful after the war, despite never realizing his dream of being a pilot.

My quest to find Jozef Kurek was a journey of the heart, but on the morning I found Jozef, I did not suspect that when the truth of Jozef became clear, it would break mine.

Shortly after I received the documents from the Dachau archivist informing me that I might contact his widow Helene Kurek, Jozef's true story began to unfold.

His residency records indicated that he had become a construction worker after his release from prison and had married Helene Brandt, a woman with two boys and a girl from a previous marriage.

I wrote Helene at the address the archivist provided, and requested a photo of Jozef. I would need my mother to confirm that this man was indeed my father, plus it excited me to think that I might be able to place, for the first time ever, a picture of a handsome, vivacious, stylish, dynamic man in our family photo album—my father.

Helene responded to me quickly. Within two weeks, I found a large brown envelope from Germany in my mailbox. I immediately knew by its stiffness that it contained the long-awaited photo of my father. I wanted to tear it open right then and there, but, afraid I might damage it, rushed up the sidewalk, flung the door open, and grabbed a knife in the kitchen, knowing it would take too long to find the letter opener in my office. I looked at the picture and my jaw dropped. I couldn't believe what I was seeing. I thought I'd be looking at a man dressed in a military uniform with a full head of thick, blonde hair, expressive eyes, and a smile that would warm my heart. I kept staring at the picture—this couldn't be my father. The man staring back at me was dressed in a white shirt, striped tie, and a dark jacket. His hair was thin, balding in front, with a few sprigs slightly raised above his otherwise short, oiled-down hair. His widely set eyes were light-colored, obviously blue, but they looked hollow. It was the way his mouth had curved into a sneer that shocked me. Helene's letter enclosing the picture stated she and Jozef had had a daughter, Angelica. The news didn't sink in; I was still in a state of shock from looking at Jozef's picture. Instead of a handsome Polish officer with an infectious smile, I saw a sullen, angry man. He couldn't be my father.

I rushed over to Mother's house, anxious to hear the words, "he's the wrong man," when I showed it to her. I handed her the picture; she squinted and then brought it closer to her face. I tried to contain my anguish as she stared stoically at the photo.

I heard my own rapid breathing as I watched her expression studying the photo, then slowly, with sadness in her voice, said, "Yes, this is Jozef."

For the first time in fifty-five years, my mother saw the man who had abandoned her and their two children.

I wondered what she thought. Did it transport her to that day he left us stranded in a squalid displaced persons' barrack? Did she remember it as if it were yesterday?

I didn't have it in me to ask. The pain on her face was more than I could bear. I sat quietly next to her and I can't remember what else we might have said to each other. All I recall was both of us struggling with the reality of that photo. The drive home was a blur.

• • •

I would have to speak with Helene if I wanted to learn more and found her telephone number in Das Telefonbuch. Since my German was inadequate I enlisted a friend who spoke it fluently. I nervously dialed her number and when she answered, I said, "Guten Tag, this is Maria Sutton, Jozef's daughter," in German, which I had pre-written on a notepad. I placed the telephone in conference-call mode to facilitate an easier translation of our conversation. My friend communicated to Helene that I'd been searching for Jozef my entire life.

Helene asked me, "Why did I take so long?"

I took a deep breath. If she only knew that I had asked myself that same question every day of my life since I'd learned of his existence.

I tried to explain patiently, and then, lightheartedly, I said, "If the Internet had been invented forty years earlier, I'd have found him much sooner."

Helene's voice was emotionless when she told me that a car had hit Jozef while he was riding his bicycle home from work on New Year's Eve. He lay bleeding by the roadside for several hours before a passing motorist spotted him. He died in a Munich hospital, after remaining in a coma and on life support for seventeen days.

I couldn't breathe or swallow from the lump in my throat. I didn't hear anything else she said. The shadow I had been chasing my entire life would remain elusive. I had so many things I wanted to ask him, so many things I needed to know. I would never have the opportunity to ask Jozef why he abandoned us.

I regained my composure and blurted out questions about Jozef's personality, character and hobbies, anything to help fill in the blanks. "Was he kind? Did he have a good sense of humor? What kind of music did he like? What were his favorite books? Did he play with Angelica and read her bedtime stories?"

There was a long, uncomfortable pause. Helene finally said, "I don't want to cause any more pain, but Jozef was a very difficult man. We led a miserable life. Jozef had a terrible temper."

I heard the words, but not really. I was still in denial.

Only later would I understand that my rejection of the facts protected my fantasy. I could still believe in the hero that was my father.

I nonchalantly told Helene that my mother had said the same thing about Jozef, and then switched the subject to Angelica. It was an awkward conversation. I dismissed her carefully chosen words: It had to be another example of Jozef being stuck in an unwanted relationship; he hadn't married Helene until Angelica was two years old; surely Jozef had been coerced into marriage.

The discrepancy between my image of Jozef and his true character obsessed me. I couldn't reconcile with the truth. There had to be some other explanation. Perhaps my instinct was right; Mother had mistakenly misidentified the man in the picture as Jozef. Her memory was not at its best, and her eyesight was also failing.

It seemed logical to request that Angelica, my half-sister, take a DNA test. She didn't hesitate, and in a few weeks I received the results.

I couldn't ignore the words on the page. Angelica and I were related; the sullen man in the photo was, indeed, Jozef, our father.

I read the report several times, with conflicted emotions. Angelica seemed to be a caring, thoughtful person, so I was happy to have her as my half-sister; on the other hand, the picture of the sullen man and Helene's words about their difficult life made me uneasy. Again, I dismissed Helene's words and the image in the photo, envisioning myself building a strong, friendly bond with Angelica.

Happy that I had another sister, I made arrangements to meet her. When she asked me what places I wanted to visit, I said I wanted to see Jozef's grave, and also Starzhausen, Wolnzach, and Gosseltshausen, places that had been important to Jozef and my mother.

Angelica wrote in an email, which I copied into my German to English translation software, "I am not interested in my father's life. You will need to find your own transportation to those places. I will take you to his grave, but that is all."

The words stung. I had visualized Angelica and I having a good time visiting those places, talking about our father, and getting to know each other. If it had been the other way around, with Angelica coming to America, I would have taken her anywhere, no matter how far away or how expensive. Starzhausen, Wolnzach and Gosseltshausen were less than twenty miles from where Angelica lived, and I didn't understand her refusal. Whenever we had visited Mary's relatives, they had graciously taken us on trips throughout Germany.

I hadn't expected or asked Angelica to do that. Her response had perplexed and hurt me. I had wanted her to be effusive, warm, and hospitable. After all, we shared the same father. When I read Angeica's harsh email, I canceled my trip.

Looking back, I can see that I overreacted. Perhaps I was insensitive, ignoring her feelings about Jozef. Still, I didn't like being dismissed and I wanted her to know it. I distinctly remember that feeling. I remember the intensity of it. Now I realize my anger may have been out of proportion, certainly misdirected; it was never meant for Angelica. It was as if all the years of not having Jozef rose up in one giant wave. I felt as if Jozef had abandoned me, again.

The trip canceled, I turned my attention to locating other family members of Jozef's in Poland, and scrutinized his POW certificate from the International Red Cross for clues.

Jozef's sister Stanislawa was the only family member he had spoken about, besides his mother. Although I knew in all probability that

Stanislawa was no longer living, I hoped she had married and had surviving children in Poland. Her last name would no longer be Kurek, which would make locating her difficult. The quickest way would be to hire a genealogist in Poland.

I Googled "genealogists in Poland" and emailed those with an English website. After corresponding a few times, I hired an excellent genealogist, Ewa, and wired her a small advance to fund the research. Within a few weeks she found them. It was too quick, too easy, and impossible not to have doubts.

To confirm that she had the right family, I instructed her to ask them three questions: (1) What was Jozef's father's name? (2) What was his sister's name? (3) Where did he work in forced labor?

Ewa telephoned a listing for Antoni Kurek in Grezowka and Elzbieta answered. They answered all three questions correctly; I had found my Kurek family!

They were overjoyed and surprised to learn they had a relative living in the United States. The genealogist, Ewa, drove up to Grezowka on a cold snowy day in January to meet them, transcribe the family history, and photograph Grezowka. When I received the family tree I was elated. Jozef had come from a large family and had many living nephews and nieces.

I sent them a large box of picture books of Colorado, and places of interest in America, photographs of myself and my family, the manuscript of my search for Jozef, and two large containers of Hershey chocolate bars. My friend Mary Lamirato's relatives always requested Hershey chocolate whenever she visited Germany. After the war, American pilots had thrown boxes of chocolates from the planes to help feed the starving Germans.

The Kureks were thrilled with my gifts and anxious to welcome me into their family. After my unsettling exchange with Angelica, I had an even stronger need to meet Jozef's family in Poland. I contacted Ewa to make arrangements for Elzbieta to come to America. Mother was in poor health and I couldn't risk leaving her for the long trip to Poland.

Elzbieta, who spoke no English asked if Justina, the granddaughter of Jozef's brother Aleksander, and fluent in English, could accompany her.

Unfortunately, the U.S. State Department denied Elzbieta's visa. She didn't meet the requirements of the immigration test: having a spouse, children, property, and a job. It was presumed she would have no reason to return to Poland and would choose to remain in America. Elzbieta lost her job with the postal service in Poland when she joined the Solidarity movement and the Polish government perceived her as a high risk. Since then she hadn't gained employment and lived with her mother and father, Antoni and Zofia Kurek.

On her behalf, I wrote letters to President George W. Bush's Chief of Staff, Secretary of State Condoleeza Rice, and to my U.S. Senators and Representative, appealing the decision, but received standardized denial letters. The Chief of Staff referred my letter to the Department of Homeland Security and months later I received a standard response, misspelling Elzbieta's name.

The State Department approved Justina's visa, however, as she was a high school student in her final year, met the presumptive immigration requirements, and was allowed to enter the United States. I paid for Justina's ticket, as the Kurek family couldn't afford the $900 airfare.

Justina, tall with blonde hair and blue eyes—a Kurek family trait that I inherited—was thrilled and grateful, lavishing me with many gifts: Polish vodka, chocolates, cookies, a few books about Poland, and many photographs and legal documents of the Kurek family. Evenings we'd pour over the birth certificates of Jozef's siblings and label each picture, placing them in my family album. As I read each document and viewed each picture, the people began taking form, becoming real, not just shadows somewhere beyond the stars of the night sky. Jozef was more than the fantasy I had of him as a daring pilot: he was a son, brother, uncle, and cousin in a flesh and blood family, who had their own struggles and triumphs. This was Jozef's family—my family, and I now had their stories.

Jozef and Apolonia Kurek residence, Grezowka, Poland, circa 1920s.

Left: Stanislawa (Kurek) Cegielka, Grezowka, Poland, 1924. Right: Jozef's brother Wladyslaw, pre-1939.

Above: Zofia Kurek, Grezowka, Poland, 1928.
Right: Stanislaw and Janina Kurek, date unknown.
Below: Aleksander and Aleksandra Kurek, Grezowka, Poland, 1922.

Jozef was the fifth and youngest child of Jozef and Apolonia Kurek. His mother was thirty-eight when he was born, and his father, an illiterate farmer, was fifty-five and died fighting for Poland's independence when Jozef was still an infant.

Jozef had two brothers and two sisters. The birth certificates of his brothers and sisters were written in Russian, Polish, or Latin, depending on which country occupied and ruled Poland at the time. Jozefs brother, Aleksander, the firstborn, was nineteen years older, and his other brother, Wladsylaw, sixteen years his senior. Stanislawa and Zofia were twelve and three years older than Jozef, respectively.

I asked Justina about Jozef's attendance at the Polish School of Eagles and she confirmed he was there, but said she had no records or other information about it. I sent an email to the school, but never received a response.

Justina didn't know very much about Jozef, but said her grandfather, Antoni, remembered him and wanted to meet me, stating that he thought I was a "very strong woman." I laughed because I've never considered myself in that light.

Justina's month-long visit went by quickly. We flew to New York City for a weekend because Justina wanted to see the Statue of Liberty. I also took her to a Broncos football game, which she enjoyed tremendously. When I explained that everyone in the stadium would stand up for America's national anthem, she declined to stand, saying her allegiance was to Poland. Half-time entertainment included a tribute to American soldiers in Iraq, and the band unfurled an American flag covering the entire football field. Four jet fighters flew low over the stadium, and then soared steeply into the sky. I caught a glimpse of Justina, her eyes brimming.

When I took Justina to the airport for the trip home to Poland, I felt I was becoming part of the Kurek family, and relieved that they were honest, hardworking people—Jozef had come from a good family, restoring my faith in him. Jozef's image once again glowed untarnished and I wanted to meet Angelica to tell her in person what a wonderful family Jozef had. Also, I had a need to see Jozef's grave.

I contacted Angelica to say I would be traveling to Germany, after all, and wanted to meet her. She assured me that she would be happy to see me, but didn't offer to pick me up at the airport or provide transportation. She informed me that a real estate shortage in Germany necessitates that graves be leased, and the lease on Jozef's grave had not been renewed—he had been removed from the cemetery.

My heart stopped beating. From the time I first learned of Jozef's death, I had wanted to visit his grave; it would be the closest I would ever get to him. I wanted to silently talk to him and thank him for giving me life. I envisioned putting a single yellow rose on his grave. I could hardly breathe, but somehow I managed to pull myself together and tell Angelica I understood.

Sometimes I still feel empty, robbed of the chance to come so close to Jozef, but I do not blame Angelica. Cemeteries in Germany are like beautiful parks and required by law to be maintained with fresh flowers and mowed grass. The ten-year leases are quite expensive, and most graves are removed after the leases expire. Knowing how Angelica and her family felt about Jozef, I'm surprised that they maintained his grave for the thirty years that they did, and I respect them for that, but I still feel an ache and emptiness to not have been able to come that close to him.

I made arrangements for private transportation and asked my daughter Cindie to accompany me for the short, three-day trip to Germany.

Angelica invited us to brunch at her townhouse in Dachau, where she, along with her daughter, Stephanie, greeted us. We walked up three flights of stairs to her apartment and were warmly welcomed by Angelica's husband, Bernard. In Europe, it is customary to kiss each cheek in greeting, but I extended my right hand. He shook it, drawing me closer and lightly kissed me on my right cheek. After toasting to our reunion with champagne, Bernard quietly left the apartment.

Angelica gave me a tour of her home and I was impressed with how well the interior had been decorated and how immaculately clean it was. I wanted to say her impeccability was inherited from Jozef, but thought it better not to broach the subject until Angelica did. She gave me an opening as we toured the kitchen. She wore dark wool socks and no shoes and pointed to the bunions on her feet. I took off my shoes and showed her mine. We both laughed and agreed Jozef was to blame for our feet.

Angelica had prepared a spectacular table full of German delicacies, enough to feed thirty people. For the occasion, Angelica gave me a large picture book of the city of Dachau, and I brought her a bouquet of fresh flowers.

As we continued to drink champagne, the translator, Renatta, Angelica's childhood friend and neighbor who spoke fluent English, created a warm, intimate atmosphere as Angelica and I began a conversation about our father.

Jozef had worked hard throughout his life, but his drinking had turned dangerous and he had continued the old card-playing habits he had acquired in the DP camps. Helene would look out the window for him every night, but he seldom went straight home from work, instead stopping by a bar to drink beer and play cards. If he won at cards, he would be in a good mood, but if he lost, then Helene and her children would suffer his alcoholic rages.

Angelica sobbed as she told me about the day she and her siblings came home from school to find Jozef drunk and furious, completely naked, kicking and beating Helene who lay writhing on the floor, sobbing and begging him to stop.

Angelica stood up now, crying uncontrollably, saying, "What Jozef did to us was not right!" She hysterically repeated the words several times, "It was not right! It was not right!"

I wanted to jump up from the couch and put my arms around her, wipe away her tears, but I clung to my image of Jozef as a good, loving father. I could only nod my head in agreement, unable to speak.

When Angelica calmed down, I told her that my mother was a deeply religious person who never spoke ill of anyone. "When I informed her how Jozef had died, my mother said, 'I hope he suffered before he died, and it is justice that he died like a dog on the side of the road.'" I didn't tell Angelica that my mother vacillated between loving and hating Jozef, sometimes in the same breath.

Angelica looked startled, but her anger returned when I said I hoped she would remember his good qualities.

Her expression hardened. "There was nothing good about Jozef." He had denigrated them frequently, referred to them as "animals" many times, and threatened to kill Helene each time she told him she wanted a divorce.

What could I possibly say in his defense? Nor did I want to. My entire body stiffened, becoming like a heavy rock. I looked away from Angelica, focusing on the floor, the words "don't fall apart" playing silently through my thoughts. Angelica left the room, returning a few moments later, and trying to manage a smile, invited us to sit at the table for the lavish meal she had prepared. Our daughters began talking and the conversation soon lightened.

After brunch, we stopped by a bakery and bought cakes and pies to take to Helene's house, where we would visit over coffee. As we drove by the Dachau cemetery, Angelica asked if I wanted to see the place where Jozef had been buried. I shook my head.

After we parked by the six-story, pale yellow concrete building with a flat roof and row-upon-row of square, austere windows, I thought of the many times Jozef had walked down this sidewalk and entered the door in which I had just passed through. I felt as if I were invading his privacy. Angelica introduced me to Helene, who was sitting on a large, overstuffed chair. She didn't rise to greet me, so I kneeled down beside her, gently touching her arm, stating through Renatta how pleased I was to meet her, before sitting down on the large sofa on the opposite wall from her chair. The room was sparsely decorated, the doors painted white, the room wallpapered with a silver pattern woven into the solid white background. Several brown, imitation Persian throw rugs had been placed at each doorway. Judging by the size of the living room, the apartment seemed to be very small. I wanted to ask Helene if I could have a tour, but decided I should wait for her to offer.

As I surveyed the room, I envisioned Jozef in it. Did he pour himself a cup of coffee and sit at the kitchen table drinking it while he read the newspaper before going to work? Did the living room look this way when he lived here? Probably not—it would have been thirty years ago and the white wallpaper would have yellowed by now; the dark rich brown sofa faded and worn. I tried not to think where Helene had laid on the floor while Jozef was kicking her.

Helene studied me as we sat across the room from each other. Her steady gaze made me uncomfortable. It was clear Helene didn't have fond memories of the man to whom she'd been married for seventeen years.

Helene told me, "I wanted to leave Jozef many times, but I was afraid of what he would do to me and my children. I often told him if he hated his life in Germany so much, he should return to Poland, or go back to the family he had abandoned."

I held my breath, waiting for Helene to finish.

"He told me his other family was worse animals than we were."

I winced, saying nothing. After a few uncomfortable moments of silence, Helene stated that Jozef had never talked about my mother, and then went on to say he told her he'd had only one daughter while in the DP camps, not two.

I wondered which daughter he had acknowledged—me or Krys—

and the realization struck me: Jozef Kurek had been the most important person to me, yet he may not have even admitted that I existed. I went out on the patio for a cigarette to calm myself. When I returned, Angelica brought out the family photo albums. Looking through them, I found a picture of Jozef in a flower garden with a smile on his face that broke my heart. I wanted to become a part of the scene and ask him the questions I had stored in my memory over the forty years: Did you ever love my mother? Did you ever think about us? Why did you leave us?

Left to right: Stephanie and Angelica Plank, me, my daughter Cindie Day, Dachau, Germany, 2006.

After cake and coffee with Helene, Angelica drove us to an Italian restaurant in Munich, where we had dinner. Our conversation was awkward. We both must have felt our initial meeting had gone badly, and we tried too hard to set it back on course, talking about light-hearted things such as restaurants and sights to see in Munich.

When we finally pulled into the hotel parking lot, we hugged each other goodbye, with promises to stay in touch. I hoped we would.

When I returned to America, I sent Angelica a thank you card and praised her house and the fabulous brunch. She gave me her new email address. I searched for just the right birthday card for her, feeling sad when most of them contained poems about sharing childhood secrets. I settled on a message that simply said, "Best wishes to my sister on her birthday."

Days passed, weeks. The scene of Angelica hysterically crying and Jozef's horrific alcoholic rages kept playing through my mind, but I continued to excuse his behavior.

I talked to Mom, hoping she would reassure me. Surely she would recount his more noble qualities.

I was shocked by what she had to say.

He had once beaten my sister with a leather belt until blood spurted because he couldn't tolerate a three-year-old sucking her thumb. He nearly smothered me as an infant for crying in my crib; it took three men to stop him.

Mom's words cut me to the core; I desperately needed to find a redeeming quality in him. I asked my mother how she could have fallen in love with such a man; her explanation was, "Jozef wasn't like that during our time at the Breitner farm."

I surmised Jozef had to learn to control his anger, or he would have been sent to the gas chamber in Dachau.

May 2008: Poland

It was my sixtieth birthday and Keith and I usually vacationed to some exotic place to celebrate special birthdays. Poland, the place of my father's birth, was my choice for this milestone. Besides wanting to meet the Kurek family, I also wanted to obtain Jozef's records from the School of Eagles. He had wanted to become one of Poland's elite aviators. I had come to believe that his alcoholic rages had to be due to the loss of his dream.

I invited about twenty members of the Kurek family to join me for dinner to celebrate my birthday in Warsaw. We were staying at the Sheraton Hotel and I made arrangements to have a private area in the dining room. The Kurek family was noticeably excited to meet me, some having traveled six hours by train to come to Warsaw for my party. They brought me heartfelt gifts: a twelve-inch tree sculpture with a gold trunk and hundreds of amber leaves; thirty-two gold coins engraved with each historic city in Poland; six blue porcelain teacups and matching teapot, made in

Poland; a large lace tablecloth handmade by Justina's mother; and many books, photographs, and narratives of the Kurek family history.

After dinner we poured champagne and I asked Elzbieta, "I wonder what my father would think of all this?"

She smiled at me. "He would be happy and proud. The circle is now complete."

No one in the Kurek family knew what happened to Jozef after 1958 when he wrote Stanislawa asking for his birth certificate because he was getting married in Germany.

We took pictures, and I asked each family member to sign the guest book with their names and addresses so we could stay in touch. We talked about our children, grandchildren, jobs, hobbies, and our lives. I learned the Kurek family was scattered throughout Poland and had a wide range of jobs and professions. I had hired Ewa to be our translator, and she did an excellent job.

When it was time to leave, I thanked everyone for attending my birthday celebration. I told them I hadn't expected any gifts; the best gift was finding them and becoming part of their family.

Some expressed concern that I would forget them.

"How could I forget a family I spent my life searching for?"

Several of them cried.

• • •

I have a sense of unconditional acceptance from the Kurek family in Poland. I feel an indefinable, innate bond with them, even though I hardly know them. Perhaps I am being naïve. They may be more enthralled with the fact that I live in America than they are with me. Trust is a two-way street. Strangers might question my motives for searching for Jozef, but I do not question why the Kureks want a relationship with me.

I felt so happy to know about Jozef and his two hundred family members living in Poland. Justina had translated my manuscript from English to Polish for the entire Kurek family, and Antoni was especially touched that I had searched for Jozef for forty-three years. At the time of my first draft, I hadn't discovered the truth about Jozef and had ended the story as the unsolved mystery of a handsome, dashing, daring, Polish officer who had disappeared in war-torn Germany and me looking at the stars of the night sky, fantasizing and searching for him.

I desperately wanted to meet Antoni—the one remaining family member who saw Jozef frequently, and remembered him.

The next day we went to Grezowka to meet Antoni and some of the relatives who were unable to attend the birthday celebration in Warsaw. Grezowka is a small, rural village about one hundred miles southeast of Warsaw that relies on agriculture for its economy. The small, wood-framed houses in the village are built close to each other and do not have lawns. Residents plant vegetable gardens in their front yards because they need the food.

As we pulled into the backyard of Antoni's house, about ten Kurek family members came rushing out of the door to greet me.

Street sign in Grezowka, Poland, identifing city limits, 2008.

Grezowka, Poland, 2008.

I was taken aback by how short Jozef's nephews, Antoni and Zygmunt, were, and they must have noticed my surprise. They explained that their father, Aleksander (Jozef's brother), was a very tall man but had married an extraordinarily short woman.

We walked around the house, and Antoni showed me the horse barn, storage shed, and neatly stacked piles of wood.

"What do you remember most about my father," I asked Antoni.

"His face—I can see it in yours. He was a lively, exciting person to be with. We used to follow him wherever he went."

I had hundreds of other questions I wanted to ask, but at that moment, I couldn't think of a single one. I took pictures, searching my mind for all those questions I had dreamed of asking Jozef, but none materialized.

One of the Kurek women came outside to let us know dinner was ready, and we began to walk slowly towards the house.

The Kurek women had spent all morning preparing a seven-course meal for me with all my favorite Polish foods: *Pierogi, Golombki* (made with the youngest, most tender cabbage leaves), pork cutlets, cucumbers and sour cream, red cabbage, young red potatoes, chicken soup with homemade noodles. They topped off the meal with a giant, four-layer birthday cake Elzbieta had made from scratch and decorated with intricate patterns. During dinner, Antoni talked about the Kurek family. Shortly after their father's death, Aleksander and Wladyslaw inherited the Kurek land. Both were married with children of their own. Jozef was a young child who spent his boyhood working on his brothers' farm. His nieces and nephews were closer to his age and wherever he went, the children would follow. He was lively, talkative, and popular with everyone.

Jozef was a restless young man who wanted more out of life. Antoni had fond memories of Jozef, describing him as a kind, thoughtful, energetic person who loved his widowed mother and took good care of her.

After dinner we went to the cemetery to place candles on the graves of each Kurek family member. When we came back to the house, Antoni played the accordion, and I gave each of them a gift from America before leaving.

The next day we would go to Deblin, home to the Polish School of Eagles and I could hardly contain myself—tomorrow I would have a good reason to forgive Jozef.

Elzbieta had arranged for one of the officers at the school to give us a private tour of the museum located on the campus. As the officer began explaining the history of the School of Eagles and pointing out the numerous artifacts and pictures of Poland's aviator heroes, he proudly compared his school to the U.S. Air Force Academy.

Prior to WWII, applicants had to complete four years of college before being accepted, but today, top high school graduates begin learning to fly within their first year, unlike the U.S. Air Force Academy in Colorado Springs that doesn't allow cockpit time until the cadet's senior year.

So far, it made sense to me and fit into Jozef's timeline: He was twenty-three at the time of Germany's invasion and would have been in his first year at the school, having completed his college education at age twenty-two.

Above: Polish School of Eagles Museum, Deblin, Poland, 2008.

I asked the officer where the pre-WWII student records were kept.

He told me, "All the records were transferred to another location when the students were being evacuated during the invasion."

More research was still ahead. We continued the tour and I thanked him for his time.

When we finished and were outside, I asked Ewa if she would obtain the records.

She gave me a puzzled look. "Your father would not have qualified to be a student at the School of Eagles, he only had a fourth-grade education."

Shocked, I searched Elzbieta's face, and when Ewa translated our conversation, Elzbieta nodded her head in agreement.

Ewa explained that none of the Kurek family had gone to college and that during Jozef's time, the area did not have any schools beyond the fourth grade. The Kurek family had a picture of Jozef in a military uniform, but speculated that during the invasion, all able-bodied young men were conscripted into the Polish army to help evacuate the School of Eagles, which was the reason that Jozef was in Deblin during the invasion and was captured.

I couldn't believe what I was hearing; I tried to maintain my composure.

We stopped for lunch and I tried to keep from breaking down by making small talk about what a beautiful country Poland was, how much I appreciated the wonderful dinner that had been prepared for me the day before, and thanked them for arranging the private tour of the School of Eagles.

It was still early afternoon, but I made an excuse that I wanted to return to Warsaw before dark. The train ride back to Warsaw was a fog. I didn't want to talk to Ewa or Keith; I pretended to sleep, my mind replaying the words, "He wasn't a pilot in the Polish Air Force."

Back at the hotel room, I collapsed. My image of Jozef was completely destroyed. Helene and Angelica and Mother were right: He was a brutal, heartless man, a liar. If his blood ran through my veins, what kind of person was I?

Keith tried to console me, but to no avail. Nothing he or anyone could say would make me feel better. I fell asleep heartbroken and exhausted. I wanted to see Jozef, to call him an evil, lying person, and ask him how he could have done what he did. I thought of all the years I had fantasized about him, the times I ached to see him and talk to him, to pour out my heart to him. I felt betrayed and a fool to have spent a lifetime searching for him; I would have been better off never having overheard that conversation on July 4, 1961.

The next morning I awoke still drained, sad. I had lost all spirit. Slowly, I began to integrate the painful truth, and in a strange, inexplicable way, I felt strengthened by it. I felt free. Since the time I had first heard the words "dirty DPs," I had felt inferior. I'd thought Jozef could give me the validation I needed. But I realized now that only I had the power to do that.

Through many wrenching months I learned that the truth, no matter how harsh and painful, is better than the unknown. The truth does set you free! My wound has healed and I am stronger now, wiser, more forgiving.

I can again thank Jozef. He had given me the greatest gift—life.

ELEVEN

A Desperate Act

Finding the truth about Jozef had been the most painful experience of my life and I was leery of what I might uncover if I found Wasyl, Mom's brother. She did not speak freely about her family and I was afraid of more family secrets that would test my sense of self. But I had promised Mother I would try to find her brother, knowing how much she loved him. I began focusing my time and energy on Wasyl, not only for Mom, but also because it would complete the puzzle of the family I never had and would make my family whole again. I hoped that Wasyl was still alive.

The search took me behind the former Iron Curtain, including Russia and Ukraine. The search for records in former communist countries kept me going in circles. I had worked with archives in the United States, Australia, Germany, and Poland, but I discovered a remarkable difference between obtaining records from Western countries and those from Eastern European ones. Of course, there is the language barrier but that was not a major obstacle in searching German records, whereas it was quite challenging in searching records in Russia and Ukraine.

Polish archivists seemed less suspicious and more responsive to requests for information than did the Russians and Ukrainians. In Poland, I could email almost any archive and receive an English response within a few days. Not so in Ukraine. They wanted formal applications for birth, marriage, and death certificates to be submitted in triplicate, typewritten in Cyrillic, and a cashier's check for seventy-five dollars for each inquiry.

Wasyl's records were located in countries that had previously been paranoid and unfriendly toward the U.S. The Ukraine Post Office returned as undeliverable most of my requests for information. I spent a considerable amount of money hiring translators since I was unable to grasp the Cyrillic alphabet.

Cyrillic alphabet for Ukrainian

Аа	Бб	Вв	Гг	Ґґ	Дд	Ее	Єє	Жж	Зз	Ии
a	b	v	h	g	d	e	je	ž	z	y
[a]	[b]	[w~v]	[ɦ]	[g]	[d]	[e]	[je / e]	[ʒ]	[z]	[ɪ]
Її	Йй	Кк	Лл	Мм	Нн	Оо	Пп	Рр	Сс	Тт
ji	j	k	l	m	n	o	p	r	s	t
[ji]	[j]	[k]	[l]	[m]	[n]	[o]	[p]	[r]	[s]	[t]
Уу	Фф	Хх	Цц	Чч	Шш	Щщ	Юю	Яя	ь	'
u	f	x	c	č	š	šč	ju	ja	ʼ	″
[u]	[f]	[x]	[t͡s]	[t͡ʃ]	[ʃ]	[ʃt͡ʃ]	[ju / u]	[ja / a]	-	

Ukrainian Cyrillic alphabet.

Most of the letters I sent to Turka, Stryj, Lviv, and the surrounding area, almost always including fifty dollars, were returned along with the money after six to seven months. A few Ukrainian organizations did respond relatively quickly, in English, but these were mostly referrals to other organizations, which I contacted to no avail.

Russia was the worst. I seldom received a response from any organization, and the few times I did, it was to inform me they had no information. Under Communism, learning the English language was discouraged. Since the failure of Communism, however, many Eastern European countries have added English to their school curriculum and younger generations are becoming more fluent in English, and more helpful as a result. During my trips to Eastern Europe, I could always count on teenagers and young adults, eager to demonstrate their English language skills, to give me information.

Obtaining the white pages of telephone directories in Ukraine from the Internet was impossible, and my research in Ukraine via emails or the Internet produced no significant results. Most people in Husne didn't have telephones and probably had never seen a computer.

My first mistake was in searching for the name "Czeczerska;" I wasted several precious weeks before it occurred to me that the Slavic language used both the feminine and masculine forms of a name. During a casual conversation with Mom, I realized I should be searching for "Czeczerski," a fact I should have known; my mother has always ended the surname of her Polish women friends with "ska" and their husbands with "ski."

No equivalent of Das Telefonbuch existed in Ukraine, but Googling the name Czeczerski was far more productive than searching for the feminine form, and I came across many websites with that spelling. I sent mass mailings to every business and individual with the name Czeczerski, but had no luck.

I then turned to immigration records in Australia, because Mom was certain that Wasyl had immigrated there. She believed the family had changed their name to "Nowak" because it was too dangerous to use their real name, so I began sending letters to anyone named "Nowak" or "Novak" in Ukraine, Poland, Germany, and Australia. The name was so common I knew it would be almost impossible to find Wasyl using that method, and by now I was aware that I had only a short amount of time left when Mom would still be with us.

For some reason, Mom had come to believe that Wasyl, his wife, and twin boys had all died in an airplane crash. I checked immigration, death, and aviation records in Australia, placed newspaper advertisements, but after several months this too ended without results.

Mom then became convinced that Wasyl had been taken to Siberia, and I began an unrelenting search for Siberian deportation records. Contacts with the Russian Embassy, International Red Cross, Jewish organizations, Church of Latter Day Saints, and countless other organizations produced nothing.

After exhaustive hours of research and hundreds of dollars spent in vain, I became frantic. My mother was eighty-seven years old and her health was deteriorating visibly every day. Time was running out: would Mom ever see her brother again?

May 2006: Moscow, Russia

The defining moment in finding Wasyl came unexpectedly during a trip to Russia. Many of our friends had warned us to be cautious in Russia, because the Russians are suspicious of Americans and would watch us closely. My husband and I never felt we were under surveillance in Moscow, nor did we feel we had to watch what we said. To the contrary, the English version of the *Moscow Times* was available in our hotel, and many front-page articles were critical of Putin's handling of domestic and foreign affairs. One of the amazing things I learned in Russia is that their World War II monuments all show the dates 1942 to 1945 as the duration of the war. When I saw this, I turned to Keith and said, "Apparently, the Russians don't consider their invasion of Poland and Ukraine in 1939 as the start of World War II!"

We found Russia to be an exotic country. The people were friendly, outgoing, and helpful; the storekeepers graciously called cabs for us, and strangers stopped to give us directions. Many Russians spoke English, and we did not have a difficult time finding our way around. The Russians had a great sense of humor and were not the stern, oppressed people I had been told about, who would be dressed in shabby clothes, wool skirts, scarves, and clodhopper shoes. The women wore the latest haute couture fashions and had trim figures. Russian cuisine was excellent, with many exotic dishes topped off with caviar.

American franchises and products could be seen throughout Moscow: McDonalds, Szbarro, and Marlboro, to name a few.

Russians preferred American dollars and Euros to rubles and I saw American dollars changing hands throughout Moscow. Japanese tourists carried U.S. dollars, as did those holding passports from around the world. When I purchased my *balalaika* from a merchant on Arabat Street, she reached into a huge leather pouch full of American twenty-dollar bills to give me my change.

Early one morning Keith and I walked to a section of the Kremlin where our group was met by our tour guide, a jovial young man who described our surroundings as Napoleon's former headquarters.

He told us, "This was where Napoleon waited for Russia to surrender, but Russia has never been defeated on its own soil."

We boarded the bus and drove by the Moscow Institute of Physics and Technology. Our guide pointed out that, "The Institute was created in 1946 and made it possible for Russia's technological advances that launched Sputnik and Yuri Gargarin's journey. Russia was the first country to launch a man into outer space."

At Pushkin Square, our guide affectionately recited the tragic life and love story of Russia's most famous poet, Aleksandr Sergeevich Pushkin. "In his youth, Pushkin's poems reflected his liberal views, which led to his exile to several places, including Odessa, Ukraine, where he had love affairs with married women. Czar Nicholas I released him from exile, leading to his acceptance by Russia's nobility and his search to marry 'the most beautiful woman in Russia.' The marriage ended in tragedy because his wife, a coquette, shamelessly flirted with royalists, which eventually led to a duel with one of her lovers. Mortally wounded, Pushkin died two days after the duel." Everyone on the tour bus was touched by this story and I felt that the Russian people are romantics at heart; my image of Russia as an "Evil Empire" softened.

Keith and I visited upscale shops such as Chanel, Escada, and Gucci, and marveled at the Ritz Carlton Hotel under construction across the street from Red Square, and the ostentatious subway system that looked more like a grand opera house or museum, the walls gilded in gold. Vendors sold vodka in every underground street crossing, yet the city was clean and the Moscow River unpolluted. We bought Russian nesting dolls on Arabat Street, saw Tolstoy's house, Yuri Gargarin's statue, ate borscht, drank vodka, and devoured American hamburgers at the Hard Rock Café.

Our tour ended at St. Basil's Cathedral, and I noted several black limousines parked in front of the Kremlin's main administrative building.

The author in front of St. Basil's Cathedral, Red Square, Moscow, Russia, 2006.

Our guide noticed, too. "Something important must be happening," he said.

Keith and I queued in the line of tourists, two city blocks long, to tour Lenin's final resting place. We stood in the pouring rain for over an hour before finally walking down the wide steps to the underground. I had expected a musty odor, but it smelled clean and fresh. Russian soldiers, dressed in their finest brown uniforms, furtively snapped their fingers to keep the procession of tourists moving through Lenin's dark, cool, underground mausoleum to view his waxen corpse. Only Lenin's green and white face and hands, highlighted with bright spotlights, could be clearly seen underneath the glass case in the eerie darkness. The mummified body, dressed in a suit, looked grotesque. I watched the guards, posted in every corner of the tomb, trying to dismiss an insane idea, but the thought persisted. The remaining tour of the Kremlin grounds became a blur with everything moving in slow motion, and I found myself walking with my husband toward the café to get coffee on that rainy day.

I couldn't concentrate on a word Keith was saying. My mind kept drifting toward a bizarre notion and I was unable to think of anything else—not even the grandeur of St. Basil's Cathedral with its brilliant red, orange, and yellow turrets could distract me from my electrifying thoughts: that the secret agents of Russia's Kremlin might somehow provide the key to finding Wasyl.

My crazy idea kept gnawing at me. The more I thought about it, the more logical it became. As a former federal investigator, I was conscious that I might need an insider to crack the Siberia deportation lists, to find out what happened to Wasyl.

During our tour of Lenin's mausoleum, it occurred to me that the Kremlin was the center of power in Russia and important records would be kept there. Russian soldiers were visible everywhere on the Kremlin grounds, and my thoughts raced: The KGB could find Wasyl!

I told Keith, "I am going to hire a KGB agent to find Wasyl."

He looked at me in disbelief.

I'd often heard there's a fine line between insanity and genius. The more I thought about hiring a KGB agent, the less preposterous the idea became. If Wasyl had, in fact, been taken to Siberia and died there, at least my mother and I would know what happened to him.

I scanned the crowded streets and restaurants of Moscow, trying to figure out who might be a KGB member.

KGB is the abbreviation for Committee for State Security, the Soviet Union's preeminent intelligence agency, whose emblem is the sword and the shield. Operating from 1954 to 1991, the agency's powers were similar to that of the U.S. Central Intelligence Agency (CIA). On December 21, 1995, then-president of Russia, Boris Yeltsin, signed a decree disbanding the KGB. The agency was succeeded by the FSB, Federal Service of Security.

However, many retired and former KGB agents advertise their investigative services on the Internet. I could hardly wait to return to Denver and start searching for a KGB agent. I knew it would be too risky to start the search in Russia. Our week-long vacation in Moscow passed quickly, but it seemed the return flight to Denver would never end. As soon as Keith and I got home, even before unpacking, I Googled "KGB Agents," and found 2.4 million websites! I spent about an hour refining my search and narrowed it down to ten agents whom I thought could do the job.

I did not feel any sense of danger about working with a KGB agent. I was a trained federal investigator and instinctively recognized warning signs when something could become perilous. I had jointly worked with the FBI on several cases and understood investigative techniques. My expectation was that the KGB operated similarly. I was desperate to find Wasyl and I felt certain that a combination of Russian greed and American money would locate my uncle.

It took several days of emails to find a retired KGB agent doing private investigative work. He wanted quite a bit of money upfront before he would start, but I felt I could trust him. I wired funds via Western Union and then held my breath.

There were no clandestine meetings on the wrong side of town, not one dimly lit smoky room. I conducted business over the Internet with the KGB agent. His email address had ".ru" at the end, confirming his location as Russia or Ukraine. He wrote in perfect English. He did not offer a contract, only a written warning not to disclose his name or his methods for obtaining the information I needed. I felt a slight twinge reading those words, but I desperately wanted to find Wasyl while my mother was still alive.

On a Friday morning I wired the fee. No confirmation came that he'd received the money. Saturday and Sunday passed with no word. I began to think I'd been conned, when an email arrived late Monday afternoon. The agent reported that he'd received the deposit and the investigation would begin the next day. I was excited but apprehensive; I was dealing with a KGB agent and had no idea to what lengths he would go to accomplish his assignment.

Within two weeks I received his initial report. It included pictures of Husne, the Czeczerski house, Anna Czeczerska, and the graves of Maria and other Czeczerski family members. I looked at the pictures for a long time, studying them. The green hills and valleys of Husne were just the way Mom had described them to me, but the picture of Anna sitting in front of a ramshackle wooden hut startled me. I was expecting an elegant, sophisticated woman sitting in front of a well-maintained country cottage instead of the haggard, weatherworn face of my aunt.

The following week the agent supplied me with a partial report containing names and dates of birth for Wasyl, Kazia, Polusia, and Anna, but withheld information about Wasyl's whereabouts until I wired the other half of the fee. The report stated that he'd found Wasyl. Relief gave way to elation when I read the words, "He is alive."

I decided that if Wasyl were in Siberia, Poland, Russia, Ukraine, Australia, or any other place in the world for that matter, I would reunite him with Mother. They had to see each other again, while they still could.

Upon receipt of the balance, I would be given Wasyl's address and telephone number. The investigative report shocked then alarmed me, giving rise to misgivings: How did the agent learn so much about the Czeczerski family in so little time?

I decided not to ask, assuming he had no motive to use corporal methods; after all, his assignment did not involve national security. With no further questions, I wired the amount due. In minutes I received Wasyl's home address, telephone number, and the Americanized spelling of his last name. I was euphoric and more than a little dazed. Wasyl resided in the United States, a few hours' plane ride away, in Bethlehem, Pennsylvania!

My hands shook as I keyed in one of the two phone numbers the agent supplied for Wasyl. I had no idea what I would say!

On the first attempt, I got a busy signal.

I tried the second number and a woman answered, Julie Marrero, Wasyl's cousin. Her father had helped Wasyl immigrate to America.

The woman seemed to know all about me. During the early part of the investigation the KGB agent had contacted Wasyl's relatives in Ukraine, and told them who I was. They had taken down my name and address and telephoned Wasyl with the news that his family was trying to contact him. They had written to me by mail but the U.S. Post Office returned their letter with an incorrect address.

I told Wasyl's cousin I had tried telephoning him on the other number. Julie asked me to wait before attempting again. "I want to be with him when you call. Wasyl has had four heart by-pass surgeries and I am worried about the stress this news might place on his heart. I will hang up the phone right now and drive straight to his house."

The next twenty minutes seemed longer than the two years I'd spent searching for Wasyl. I paced the kitchen floor, watching the large clock on the wall of the family room, waiting to call him. I stepped outside to get some air and catch my breath, constantly checking my wristwatch for the time.

I swung back and forth on the swing underneath the huge oak in our backyard, gazing at brilliant golden daisies. Was my mission coming to a close?

Calmness descended and I made my way back to the house, sat on a kitchen chair, and reached for the phone. My hand trembled and my heart raced, knowing that Wasyl would answer this time.

I heard a dial tone, then a ringing signal and, at last, a man's voice saying, "Hello?"

"Am I speaking to Wasyl Czeczerski?"

The voice eagerly replied, "Yes!"

His tone was soft, gentle, just what I'd expected. All the memories Mother had shared with me about her childhood in Ukraine came flooding back. This voice was the same person who had roamed the green hills and valleys of Husne with my mother; the person who had saved her life.

I gripped the telephone and told him who I was and the purpose of my call.

"Oh my God, my God … I have searched for my sister my entire life! I placed ads in Ukrainian, Polish, Jewish, German, and French newspapers looking for her … Oh my God!" And then he cried.

This grown man crying moved me deeply, but I remained calm and silently listened to his muffled sobs.

I told him, "My mother loves you very much, and we have been searching for you for a long time! I wanted to give my mother this gift, of finding her brother for her."

Wasyl and I spoke for a few more minutes and I told him my mother would telephone him.

I sped toward Mom's house, anxious to give her the momentous news. I don't remember what streets I took, or actually driving the car. The time passed in a hazy blur and before I knew it, I was rushing up the old porch stairs two at a time. I barely got the keys in her door.

Mom was resting on her recliner and glanced up, smiling, when I entered the house. I knelt down in front of her.

"Mom, I've got the greatest news in the world."

She looked at me intently, waiting.

"I've found him—I've found Wasyl!"

There was a long, anxious pause. Her lower lip quivered. "Is he alive?"

I nodded yes.

"Where is he? Can I see him?"

"Yes, yes, and yes. I have his phone number, he lives in Pennsylvania, and you can talk to him right now!"

"What will I say?"

"Anything you want to."

Mother thought about it for only a moment. "I'm going to tease him," she said, smiling, "the way I did when we were children."

Her first word to him was "Wasyl?"—and then her entire face lit up and her eyes glistened as she became immersed in a conversation with him.

I couldn't understand the Polish she spoke, but I studied her face—at times it was joyful, other times sad—and I knew they were talking about what had become of their lives during and since the war.

They talked for over an hour and when Mother finished the phone call, she fell silent for the rest of the day, staring into time and space. I didn't press her to tell me everything about Wasyl; she was deep in her own thoughts, and I didn't want to disturb her.

Later that evening I asked her what she was thinking.

Mom smiled. "I wonder what he looks like now."

Upon returning home, I asked Julie Marrero's daughter to email me some photos of Wasyl. She sent one of him at age twenty-one and I was shocked. Mom had carried two pictures of her family with her to America: one of a young man she'd said was her brother, and the other a portrait of her parents, Maria and Mihas. I had enlarged and framed both, believing they were my uncle Wasyl and my grandparents.

The photo I received looked nothing like the man in the picture my mother had given me.

The next morning I drove to her house, bringing the three pictures with me. When Mom gazed at the photo, a warm expression and smile crossed her face. Her eyes filled. "Yes, this is my brother."

I gently pulled out the other pictures she had brought with her to America and quietly asked her who they were.

"I got these from a childhood friend while I was living in the Rosenheim DP camp. I didn't recognize the people in the pictures but my friend assured me that people changed considerably during the war. I felt people could not change that much; my mother had dark brown hair, not blonde. But I accepted my friend's explanation and kept the pictures, believing they must have been my brother, mother, and stepfather, whom I had not seen in such a long time."

I was dumbfounded. Over the decades, Mother and I would look at those photos of strangers and she'd tell me stories about her beloved brother Wasyl. I had even sent the picture out in mass mailings to people named Czeczerski or Nowak in Australia, Poland, Ukraine, Germany, and the United States.

It is beyond my comprehension how my mother could keep sixty-five-year-old pictures and tell emotional stories about the people in them, not knowing for certain that they were her family. I concluded the war had traumatized her, and she wanted to believe they were her family; she needed these photos if she wanted to keep her memory of them alive. Or perhaps the truth would have been too painful. Or maybe she was too proud to admit her friend had deceived her.

I don't know. But I believe the truth has a way of emerging and those pictures are a good example. I became suspicious when my mother's memory first started fading. Whenever I brought the photos out in recent years, she told me she had no idea who the people were, and I ignored her remarks, attributing it to her failing memory. Looking back, it was another example of how she no longer remembered the many stories she had spun over the years. Whether it was to protect herself, or me, I'll never really know. I never got a satisfactory answer when I questioned her about it. And now, it didn't seem important. We had found Wasyl.

I mailed off photos of Mom, and when Wasyl saw her immigration picture from 1951, he immediately recognized her by the beauty mark on her face.

I began making arrangements for their reunion. Wasyl was unable to travel to Denver because of his heart condition. My mother had severe, disabling arthritis; she used a walker for short distances and was generally confined to a wheelchair. Still, we decided Mother was strong enough to make the trip to Bethlehem.

My next decision was the duration of the visit. Should it be a few days, weeks, a month? After all, they hadn't seen each other for sixty-five years, and, at their age, it could be their one and only reunion. I thought about it for a number of days. Mom didn't like to leave the comfort of her home for any length of time—about three hours each week for our Sunday drives up into the mountains satisfied her, anything longer made her tired and agitated. I didn't know what effect sleeping in a strange bed so far away from home would have on her health. Finally I just asked her how long she wanted to visit Wasyl. She thought about it for a few minutes then said, "I think a weekend would be nice." I made reservations for us to fly out on Saturday morning and return Tuesday afternoon. If Mom did well on the trip, we could visit Wasyl again for possibly a longer time next spring.

When friends and colleagues heard about the pending reunion, they encouraged me to contact the news media. I was initially reluctant; I wanted their reunion to be a private time between a brother and sister who loved each other deeply—I didn't want cameras intruding on the sanctity of that moment. But I came to the realization that thousands of people were searching for their lost families and many had given up hope. Our story could give those people renewed faith.

Mother and Wasyl agreed without hesitation that such an important story should be made public.

My mother had always been fond of Adele Arakawa, a local news anchor for Denver's NBC affiliate, and their station seemed the logical choice for the job. I contacted the news department and they promised to send a reporter to interview us.

My initial enthusiasm turned to concern when I realized I would probably be asked how I had found Wasyl. I was hesitant to disclose that I'd used a KGB agent, for two reasons: the agent had directed me not to divulge his name or methodology, and as a senior level manager with the federal government, my using a former cold-war enemy might be frowned upon in Washington, D.C. I discussed my concerns with my supervisor and he assured me he didn't foresee any repercussions from my employer.

A Channel 9 news van arrived and an excited young reporter, carrying a large camera, surveyed my house for just the right place for the interview. He decided on my office and began setting up lights and umbrellas toward the back corner, facing the computer and library, for the interview. He seemed impressed by my bookshelves full to overflowing with research binders. The reporter interviewed Mother and me for three hours!

The two most important questions were: Why did I want to find Wasyl? And, how did I find him? I went ahead and told him the truth, and the KGB angle intrigued him. He filmed several minutes of me Googling "KGB Agents" and scheduled another interview with us after we returned from meeting Wasyl in Bethlehem.

Our flight from Denver to Newark left early in the morning. It was still dark when we pulled up in front of Mom's house, but she had turned on the porch light and I could see her silhouette standing at the front door waiting, dressed and ready to fly the seventeen hundred miles to see her brother.

United Flight #912 touched down at Newark Liberty Airport, and the pilot announced that our flight represented a historic occasion for one of the passengers: Julia Venckus, who had made the trip to be reunited with her brother whom she had not seen in sixty-five years. The entire cabin erupted in cheers and applause; each passenger congratulated Mom as they disembarked the plane.

We had informed the press in Bethlehem of our schedule, but asked that they limit their coverage to after Wasyl and Mother's first meeting.

The extraordinary reunion took place in the privacy of my mother's hotel room. My sister Krys, Julie Marrero, and I waited in an adjoining room, the door left slightly open so that if Wasyl or Mom needed us, we could immediately respond.

Mom sat in her wheelchair. The door to her room was ajar for Wasyl.

Finally, a frail Wasyl entered and Mom teased, "Hey, what are you doing here?"

Wasyl reached out for her and replied, "So here you are. I look for you for sixty-five years, and here you are."

Those were their first words spoken to each other face-to-face since 1942. They kissed and gently embraced, and Wasyl handed Mom a gift: a diamond and sapphire pendant on a delicate white-gold chain, a gift he probably couldn't afford but purchased for her "to make up for all the lost birthdays and Christmases."

Wasyl was eighty-five years old and Mom was eighty-eight. Years and history had separated them, but nothing and no one had broken their bond, neither Hitler nor Stalin, the war, or the ravages of time. They had each suffered their own personal tragedies and had lived separate lives, but they still cared deeply for each other, even after all that time.

They talked quietly together for more than half an hour. I heard them giggling quite often. Although I was anxious to meet Wasyl, I didn't want to interrupt their first meeting and contentedly beamed each time I heard their laughter.

Finally, I heard Mom calling me and I rushed into their room. Krys had agreed that after Mom, I should be the next one to meet him. Looking at his face for the first time, I saw the resemblance between Wasyl and Mom and knew I had found my family. I sat next to my uncle on the bed, put my arms around him, and softly kissed him and told him I loved him.

We talked for a few minutes and then I opened the door for Krys and Julie. Later, we went to the lobby where Krys's and my children were anxiously waiting to meet the great-uncle they had never met.

We popped champagne and toasted to our newfound family. I presented Wasyl with my gift to him: a gold-embossed photo album with hundreds of pictures of Mother from 1951 to the present—birthday celebrations, weddings, baptisms, vacations, Christmases—her life.

The next morning, we attended service at the Ukrainian Greek Catholic Church. Reporters quietly stood in the back. When the Mass ended, they took several pictures, and then joined about thirty of Wasyl's and Mom's friends and relatives for brunch at Bethlehem's Sheraton Hotel.

After brunch we drove to the cemetery to place flowers on the grave of Anna, Wasyl's wife of forty-four years. Wasyl said a silent prayer and touched her headstone before leaving the cemetery.

Camera crews from Bethlehem's independent TV station, as well as the photographer and reporter from *The Morning Call,* joined us at Wasyl's house. The TV reporter asked Wasyl how it felt to be reunited with his sister.

After a moment of silence, Wasyl stated, "It's nice, but it is too late. We are both old people now."

His response devastated me. "It's not too late!" I shouted, surprised by the intensity of my tone.

Wasyl and Mother silently stared at me, ignoring my outburst.

After asking more questions, the reporters wanted to film us having a conversation. We talked about many things, and I learned that the first car Wasyl ever owned was a 1950 Dodge. He was not a Steelers or Eagles fan; he preferred baseball. For most of his life, he had been employed as a steelworker for Bethlehem Steel, retiring in 1983, having benefited from his experience as a bricklayer rebuilding Germany after the war.

Wasyl said, "There was an opening for a better position at Bethlehem Steel and I decided to apply. I competed with eight other men who had more seniority. The supervisor had us all in one room. Whoever could cut a brick to fit into a certain space the best would get the job. When it was my turn to cut the brick, I used the skills I learned in Germany and I got the job."

It saddened me to hear that Wasyl, the goodhearted boy from Husne, who had dreams of becoming the president of Ukraine, had spent his life working the difficult and dangerous job of a steelworker, toiling in temperatures ranging from 2300 to 2700° F at times. But Wasyl was proud to have had a good job in America.

The reporter from WFMZ-TV left at four in the afternoon to get the film ready for airing on the evening news. We leafed through photo albums and watched the tape from a trip to Husne, taken by Julie Marrero's daughter for Wasyl; she had recorded an hour-long Greek Catholic Mass in Husne's Church, footage of Husne's beautiful vistas, and Wasyl's relatives singing, dancing, and celebrating.

We stayed to watch our story being played on TV. The reporter did an outstanding job intermingling WWII film clips with Wasyl's and Mom's statements about their capture and separation by Nazi soldiers.

Wasyl told us, "As soon as I arrived in America, I wanted to write our mother to let her know I had a good job and a place to stay. I was afraid the Communist government might intercept the letter and cause trouble for her and the rest of the family, or worse, deport them to Siberia for having next-of-kin living in the United States. I decided not to jeopardize Maria's safety by disclosing my location."

Paranoia over Russia and the atrocities committed by Stalin ran deep, and, as much as Wasyl longed to comfort his mother with the knowledge he was safe and happy, he felt he could not take that risk. The last time he'd seen his mother she'd been sobbing as German soldiers escorted him from their Husne home.

Mother and I and the rest of our family listened as Wasyl began narrating his story of the Third Reich.

TWELVE

Wasyl's Story

My husband Keith has many aunts, uncles, and cousins whom we saw each time we visited his parents in Iowa. Many of them would drop by to say hello and we would sit around the kitchen table while they told their stories. Their memories always returned to the time they served America in WWI and II—clearly the most important event of their lives. Aunt Ida recalled with sadness that the love of her life died in battle during WWI and that is why she never married. Uncle Claude served in both wars, and Uncle Curtis in WWII and the Korean Conflict. Uncle Ed vividly remembered Pearl Harbor and seeing a bomb drop into the smokestack of his ship, the *U.S.S. Arizona,* instantaneously bursting it into flames and sinking below the waters of the harbor. After the war, Ed attended college on the G.I. Bill, becoming the first member of the family with a college degree, which led to a successful career outside of farming.

Now, I, too, had an uncle whose stories I could listen to about the event that changed his life.

After the reporters left we moved into the kitchen. I brought out my writing tablet and began taking notes. I wanted to solve as many mysteries and discrepancies as possible.

Wasyl had been captured in the spring of 1941 while tilling a section of farmland about five hundred yards from the Czeczerski house. When he saw the armed soldiers he surrendered, knowing he'd be shot if he tried to run. The soldiers allowed him to say goodbye to his mother Maria. As soon as he walked through the door with the soldiers, Maria's face turned white and she started sobbing. Wasyl reached for her hand to kiss it, but the soldiers shoved him away. Kazia, Polusia, and Anna started screaming; Maria said, "Goodbye my dear son."

"I walked from village to village in a torrential downpour while the Germans rounded up every able-bodied man and woman. By the time we got to the train station, my wooden shoes had splintered and split, and my feet were blistered and bloody.

"The train was tightly packed. Hay had been spread on the floors, but there wasn't any room to sit or lie down to sleep. A bucket hung on a rope, crossing the full length of the car. We were expected to use it to relieve ourselves. It overflowed quickly, drenching us.

"The train stopped in Lviv, where the Red Cross fed us and then the Nazis escorted us into a large camp enclosed by a wooden fence. I could see St. George Cathedral from the compound. I sat against the fence and stared at the church, thinking about what would happen to me, Julia, Maria, and my younger sisters.

St. George Cathedral, Lviv, Ukraine, date unknown.

"I leaned farther back against the fence, and it gave way to a few loose and broken boards. A guard came toward me, so I calmly sat against the fence until he was out of sight, then slid underneath the broken boards and made my way to St. George Cathedral. By now it was nighttime and the doors were locked. I kneeled down on the concrete steps and began to pray. I have no idea how long I knelt there, praying, but I sensed soldiers standing in the shadows the entire time. Eventually, they came out of the darkness and escorted me back to the holding pen.

"I had digestive problems from drinking coal-blackened water and eating breadcrumbs of chestnuts, sawdust, and rye. They took us to a death camp, somewhere in a wooded area. It had five chimneys spewing smoke.

"They gave us a tour, taking us inside a large gray building and showed us the gas chambers and incinerators. The Nazis said if we caused any trouble we would end up in the gray building.

"When I saw the gas chambers and incinerators, I didn't know whether I would live to see another day. They gave me a new set of clothes: a shirt, trousers, and underwear. Our lice-infested clothes were thrown into the incinerator.

"They assigned me to the Honlley farm in Mittelbuch. Frau Honlley gave me a bowl of soup at a small table in the corner of the kitchen; I gulped it down each time she refilled the bowl, thinking it would be the only food I would get. When she served the main meal, I was too full to eat it!"

"What was the Honlley family like?" I asked, wanting to know if he had been mistreated.

"They had three sons and two daughters. All three sons had died during Germany's war: One son was killed in Russia, another taken as a prisoner of war by France and died during captivity, and the youngest was missing in action and has never been found. Jozef Honlley had lost his leg during WWI, and the family desperately needed someone to keep the farm going."

Wasyl smiled as he recalled, "Honlley's daughter fell in love with me. She was ten days older than I, and often snuck into my bedroom, which adjoined hers.

"I worked nineteen hours a day at the farm, but Jozef Honlley was generous with his food.

"When I got settled, I wrote letters to our mother Maria, and she wrote me that Julia had also been captured and taken into forced labor. Mother gave me the address of the Breitner farm, and I wrote many letters to you, Julia, but I never received a response."

Mom told him, "I never received any letters from you," speculating that Hermania must have destroyed them.

I sat with them in Bethlehem puzzling over this mystery. Since Mother and Jozef were the ones who walked to Wolnzach to get the Breitner mail, it is hard to understand why Mother would claim she never received Wasyl's letters, unless they were destroyed in transit, which doesn't make sense; there was no difficulty between Wasyl and his mother corresponding. Perhaps Jozef destroyed Wasyl's letters, but what would be his motivation? I could only speculate that my mother did receive Wasyl's letters, because she seemed to know quite a bit about his whereabouts. She may not have wanted to hurt his feelings by admitting she had received his letters but never wrote back. I had gently asked Mom many times why she had never written to Wasyl, but she adamantly stuck to her story that the letters were never received.

Pensively, Wasyl said, "I never gave up trying to contact you. I had no way of knowing it would be sixty-five years before I would talk to you again."

"What did you do after the war, Wasyl?" my mother asked.

"I was not allowed to listen to the radio or receive updates on Germany's war efforts. I only knew the war had ended because German soldiers were fleeing into the American zone, not wanting to be captured by the French army.

"One night, while eating dinner, Honlley said to me, 'The war is over. What will you do now?'

"I didn't say anything, then Honlley said, 'I could use you.'

"I thought about it, thanked him for his offer, and continued to work on the farm. I seriously considered marrying Anna Honlley and beginning a new life in Germany.

"I stayed at the farm until 1946. At the age of twenty-four I suddenly realized I was free, so I left for Biberach.

"I wanted to go home, but Maria's letters warned me of the situation in Husne and begged me not to return until they knew the full impact of Russian rule. Two of Maria's cousins, one a schoolteacher in Stryj, had already been deported to Siberia and she feared the entire Czeczerski family would be sent there, or murdered. Her cousin Wasyl Ilnytsky, a member of the insurgency, had been beheaded. Soviet officials hung his head from a wooden post placed in the center of town for two weeks, as a warning to potential insurgents. At the end of the two-week public viewing, the officials notified his widow to remove his head for burial.

"I stayed in Germany for five years after the war, but I didn't go to the DP camps because I was lucky enough to find a job. My first job was with the UNRRA, unloading army trucks filled with boxes of food for distribution to the DP camps. I worked there for two years. After that, I worked for a French company disassembling Germany's bomb manufacturing equipment. The Germans had built their underground munitions plant in a forest on the outskirts of Biberach. French soldiers disassembled the equipment and I placed the parts in boxes and loaded them into French army trucks for transport to France. I did this for about a year before deciding to learn a trade.

"I went to work for a French construction company as a bricklayer. I worked there for a year, from 1949 to 1950, laying bricks for houses and factories. I remembered the time I had helped my father build a storage shed out of large boulders the two of us had hauled from the Carpathian Mountains, using sand and lime for mortar, and decided I wanted to become a bricklayer.

"I never got the letter from my mother letting me know it was safe to return home. Eventually, I didn't receive any letters from Maria until 1957, when my wife Anna convinced me it would be safe to write Maria because many of her friends had written their families in Ukraine without repercussions. I worried about her and my sisters, knowing how dangerous Soviet occupation could be. During the 1930s, Stalin deported over 300,000 Ukrainian families to Siberia, and murdered our military and civic leaders, scientists, teachers, and other professionals. He even ordered factories to pollute Ukraine's drinking water. Families owning more than twenty-four acres of land were considered high risk for a revolution, and were exiled to Siberia. Men, childless women, and unmarried girls became slave workers in mines and large industries."

Wasyl told us, "Ukrainians openly defied Soviet policies, and burned their own homes rather than surrender to Communist authorities, refusing to harvest their crops, allowing them to rot in the fields. In retaliation, Stalin ordered an extreme increase in the mandatory quota of food to be shipped out of Ukraine, and then sealed off Ukraine's borders to prevent any import of food. The Soviet police went house-to-house, seizing whatever food had been stored. They poked the ground with their bayonets, looking for hollow spots where food had been concealed. If they found hidden food, the entire family would be dragged out of their house and shot on the spot. Anyone caught stealing food from any of the protected granaries could be shot or imprisoned for not less than ten years.

"Ukrainians ate leaves, grass, frogs, mice, snakes and birds—whatever they could find to keep from starvation. Still, an estimated three to six million Ukrainian's died of starvation from 1932–1933.

I fought for Ukraine's independence when I was a boy of fifteen; after World War II, everything was lost again. I knew I couldn't go back to Ukraine, so I started filling out applications to immigrate to Australia, Canada, or America. My cousins in America convinced me to immigrate here; they would give me a place to stay until I found a job. While I waited for the applications to be processed, I traveled throughout Germany. Wherever I went, I asked about you, Julia."

Mother said nothing. Wasyl grew silent. We sat in silence also, not knowing what to say. After a few moments, Wasyl turned to Mother and said, "Why don't you ask me about Husne or ask what happened to our friends?"

I looked at my mother to see if her face revealed anything—it did not. Anytime I had asked her that same question, why she never talked about her family, friends, or homeland, she nonchalantly shrugged her shoulders and said, "I don't know." I always felt that the pain of the losses was too much for her to bear, so she protected herself by severing herself from that part of her life.

I thought about the comment Wasyl made regarding his immigration application to Australia. During the search for Wasyl, Mother had

Left: Wasyl Czeczerski (Chichersky), Biberach, Germany, 1948.
Right: Wasyl Czeczerski (Chichersky), Mittelbuch, Germany, 1947.

told me he had immigrated to Australia and that I should check the records there. After hearing Wasyl's comment that he had applied to Australia, I surmised Mom had, in fact, received his letters, but never responded. I didn't want to ask her.

After an awkward silence, Mother began teasing Wasyl about their childhood: the mud pies she made and forced Wasyl to eat, fishing in the stream in Husne, and skiing down the slopes of the Carpathian Mountains. They talked as if they had seen each other every day.

Wasyl spoke Ukrainian to Mother, she Polish to him.

Wasyl was not surprised to hear that she had become a nurse.

"I often thought of contacting hospitals and nursing associations to find you. You had a reputation in Husne as a caring person from the time you were a little girl, with an innate ability to comfort the sick."

After dinner Wasyl brought out many photos, including their wedding album. As we turned the pages and reminisced, Wasyl seemed sad. "When I am gone, all these albums Anna put together will be thrown out. We have no children."

I told him, "I'd be honored if you gave the albums to me." Wasyl smiled, looking relieved.

The next morning, we stopped by the lobby to pick up the newspaper; a photo of Wasyl and Mother was on the front page of *The Morning Call*! The reporter wrote a wonderful article about their lives, the search, and the reunion.

After breakfast, we visited the historic downtown area of Bethlehem to buy souvenirs and books. We circled Main Street several times hoping to find parking, when a bellman flagged us down at the front entrance of Bethlehem's historic hotel because he recognized Mother. He ran into the hotel, returned with the newspaper, and asked her for her autograph. He allowed us to park in the "No Parking" valet area.

When we finished buying our souvenirs, we headed to Wasyl's house for some more time with him. Wasyl greeted us at the door,

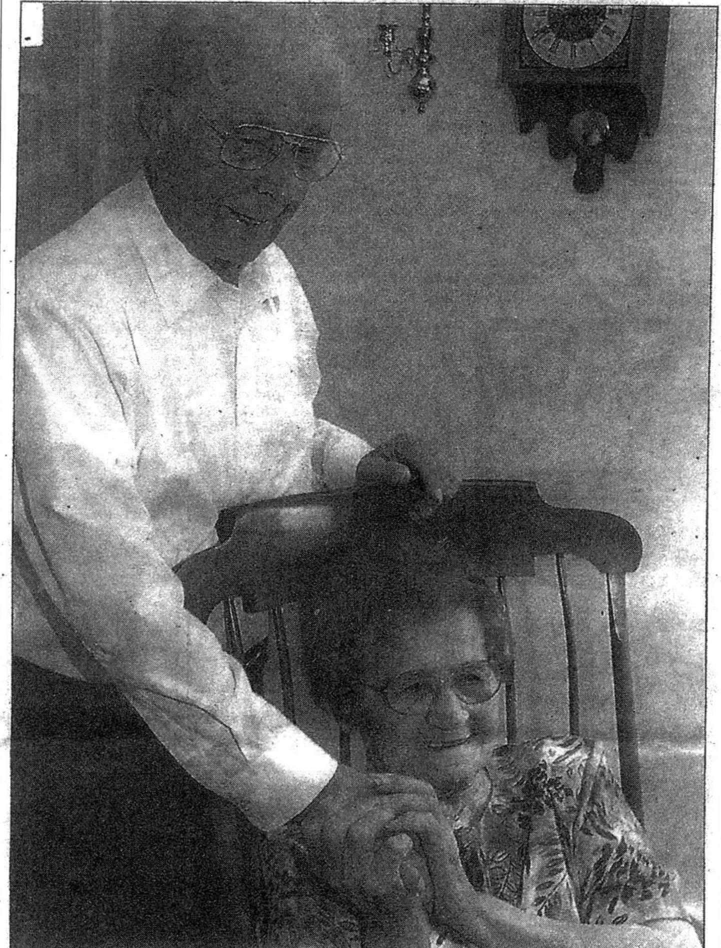

"Here you are. I look for you for 65 years, and here you are."

WASYL CHICHERSKY

Demetra Stamus Special to The Morning Call

WASYL CHICHERSKY, 85, of Bethlehem Township, and his sister Julia Venckus, 87, of Denver, Colo., spend time together Sunday. To find Wasyl, Julia's family hired an ex-KGB agent to track him down.

Divided by war, reunited in time

Mom and Wasyl on the front page of Bethlehem's local newspaper, *The Morning Call,* October 2006.

happy to see us. Our two days together had been a whirlwind of visits with friends, relatives, neighbors, reporters, and cameramen.

The morning of our departure was gray, foggy, and rainy. The mood in the house matched the weather.

In his gentle way, Wasyl told me, "You know, Maria, I am not happy that you used a KGB agent to find me." He proceeded to tell me stories of torture and murder of his friends at the hands of the KGB.

I replied, "I did what I had to do. Time was running out. We were desperate to find you."

As we put on our jackets to leave, Wasyl turned away to conceal his tears. We had delayed our departure for as long as possible. We said our goodbyes and Wasyl watched from the doorway as we took Mother to the van in her wheelchair and lifted her inside. We drove away waving to Wasyl, tears streaming down his face.

Mom and her brother Wasyl in his house in Bethlehem, Pennsylvania, on departure day, October 2006.

THIRTEEN

Maria Czeczerski

I had now found my family and had pieced together their stories. But one mystery remained that I thought would forever stay unsolved. I received that truth unexpectedly, and it became a priceless gift to my mother. That final secret was revealed during my trip to Ukraine, to meet my new maternal family. I had to see my mother's homeland, its green hills, stacks of hay, and the dirt cellar where she had hidden during WWII, waiting for soldiers to leave. Visiting Ukraine would make me feel I was home, at last. I never expected to uncover an extraordinary secret.

July 2009: Dnieper River, Ukraine

Brilliant gold domes on top of lush, dark green hills could be seen in the distance as we neared the port in Kiev. The hot, gleaming sun was no match for the glittering cathedrals and palaces crowned with elliptical roofs of gold.

Keith and I had been on Ukraine's major river for two weeks and our guided tour was coming to an end, but a new journey would soon begin—I would be meeting my Czeczerski relatives in Lviv, just a short flight from Kiev, and would finally see the green hills and valleys of the place my mother called her childhood home.

The last two weeks had been spent underneath the clear blue skies and dark, starry nights of Ukraine, gently swaying in a forward motion up the wide river. As we neared the port, we saw ostentatious mansions whose architecture rivaled the American estates of the Rockefeller's, Vanderbilt's, and Ford's. Our tour guides informed us they belonged to Ukrainian oligarchs. I wanted to see as much as I could of this ancient land for which my relatives had died for its freedom. We had traveled to the Crimea, where Catherine the Great had defeated Tatars, Mongols, and Ukrainians to give Russia access to trade with Istanbul and Greece, the place Russians call "the playground of the Czars." We saw the Swallow's Nest, a magnificent white marble castle built on top of a steep, rugged cliff overlooking the Black Sea, and had walked in the footsteps of Stalin, Roosevelt, and Churchill as they made their way to the highly polished, elaborately carved round table at Czar Nicholas' summer palace to sign the Yalta Agreement.

Further up the Dnieper, we stopped at Zaporizhzhya, where Cossacks gave a stunning show of their horsemanship and bravery. I thought of them attacking Russian tanks on horseback, then fleeing into the deep forests.

For all the wonderment and beautiful sites in this country, I could hardly wait to meet my new-found maternal relatives, the main purpose for my trip to Ukraine. By now, the wrapping on the presents I had carefully hand-carried from Denver to Frankfurt, Bucharest, Odessa, Yalta, and Kiev, by airplane, taxi, bus, and ship, had crinkled and torn, the ribbons smashed, withered, and drooping. When we got to the hotel, I placed them on the large, oval table in our suite, fluffing up the ribbons before I jumped in the shower to get ready to meet my Czeczerski family.

When the doorbell rang, I excitedly rushed to open it—and there they were—the cousins in whose faces I saw my mother. After hugs and kisses, we opened the bottles of champagne and I presented each of them with their gifts from America. They, too, had brought presents for Keith and me: hand-crafted carved wooden boxes, table runners, jewelry, and a large picture book of the Orange Revolution in Ukraine. Afterwards, we had an elaborate meal in the hotel's dining room, and then returned to the suite for our goodbyes for the night. One of my cousins said, "Maria always prayed for Julia. Ukrainians recite two different prayers: one for the living, another for the souls of those who have passed. Maria's prayers for Julia were always for the living; in her heart, she always knew that her daughter was still alive."

The next day Volodymyr, Maria's grandson, and his son, Roman, who speaks fluent English, would take us to Husne.

It was a sunny morning and I stood on our second floor balcony, overlooking the city center of Lviv, drinking coffee and imagining Mother strolling on the promenade through the park with its large bronze statues scattered in between gigantic trees that provided shade throughout the city center. Lviv had been Mother's favorite childhood place to visit and she had told me she loved to go window shopping, play in the parks, and read a good book while sitting on one of the many park benches under a shady oak. I saw Volodymyr's car pulling into the parking space and rushed downstairs to meet him. Keith and I piled into the back seat and began our long drive to Husne. As we drove down the narrow, winding road, talking about family, Volodymyr grew silent, as if contemplating whether or not to tell me something. We had talked about my grandmother Maria the night before, his memory of her being a kind, gentlewoman who always had homemade candy for the children of Husne. He seemed hesitant, groping for words, then began her story, which Roman translated for me:

"Your grandmother Maria was a beautiful woman. She was a tall, slender girl with chestnut hair and dark brown eyes. Her eyes always sparkled—she was lively and energetic—she loved to dance. She was one of the most popular girls in the small village.

"Maria was fourteen when she and her two younger sisters were orphaned. Her mother was only forty years old when she died. Her two younger sisters were sent to live with relatives, but Maria was considered old enough to work.

"The arch-priest of Holy Trinity Church in Husne, Mikhailo Treshnevsky, offered her a home and employment as a servant to the church and his family. This was considered prestigious, giving Maria a higher social status than the household servants of affluent families.

"Maria had a quiet dignity about her, and performed her church duties with elegance and grace: making communion wafers, polishing the chalice, and helping to prepare for baptisms, weddings, and other church functions. Parishioners were struck by her beauty and warmth.

"Alexander, the arch-priest's oldest son, was especially captivated. Alexander stole away from his ordination studies to spend time with her, under the pretense of needing help with his lessons. They walked the hills and valleys of the Carpathians, reciting psalms, philosophizing about the wonders of nature, happy to be with each other.

"Mikhailo had two other sons, but he wanted his eldest to follow in his footsteps and become a priest. Alexander descended from a long line of priests, including his maternal grandfather, Roman Pasechinsky.

"When the Greek Catholic Archdiocese transferred Mikhailo to Krasne, Mikhailo asked Maria to relocate with him and his family to the new church, St. Makovei. He knew her kind and good nature could be instrumental in getting the parishioners in Krasne to accept him as their new priest.

"Maria agreed and moved to Krasne with the Treshnevsky family, continuing her friendship with Alexander. Their childhood affection developed into a deep and passionate love, and, at the age of twenty-four, Maria became pregnant with Alexander's child—Julia, your mother."

The news was a bombshell to me. I had known Mihas was Mother's stepfather and that the only information she had about her biological father was that he had been a medical doctor who had died of a heart attack when she was an infant of three months. Mother didn't even know his name. When I asked Wasyl about my mother's father, he, too, did not have information, but confirmed he had been a physician and died of a heart attack while crossing a barbed-wire fence on his way home from making a house call late at night.

I had sent an email to Ukraine's Health Ministry requesting a list of medical doctors serving the Lviv region from 1910–1920, but never got a response. When I received Mother's birth certificate, the father's name had been left blank, so I knew something was not quite right, and had placed her father on my list of mysteries to solve.

I thought about the irony: neither Mother nor I knew the identity of our fathers, and neither of our birth certificates had listed the father's name. Had I not overheard that conversation during that Fourth of July picnic in 1961, I would have gone to my deathbed not knowing who my biological father was. I have known several people who discovered late in life that their aunt or sister was really their mother. A good example is Jack Nicholson, the Oscar-winning actor, who discovered at age thirty-seven that his parents were really his grandparents, and the woman he thought to be his sister was actually his mother. They took the secret to their deathbeds and Nicholson could only confirm the truth when his other sister acknowledged the facts of his birth. It had a profound effect on him; interviews with his close friends indicate he still struggles with the revelation to this day. I speculate his struggle is not with the truth, but that two people he loved and trusted deceived him. In my own case, since the day I discovered Jozef, I became skeptical of many things my mother told me, always needing to corroborate information from several different sources before I could accept it as truth.

"Are you sure Alexander Treshnevsky is my mother's father?" I asked Volodymyr.

"Yes, when Maria was dying, she told the family."

I said a silent prayer and thank you to Grandmother Maria.

"How far is Krasne from Husne?"

"Not far, less than thirty miles north of Husne, on the way. Do you want to stop there?"

"Yes!"

In about thirty minutes we pulled off the main highway onto a gravel road. We wound our way into the valley and then, as I surveyed the vistas, I could see a large church with white domes shimmering in the sunlight. We parked the car at the foot of the hill and walked the steep slope to the church. As we passed the cemetery, we stopped by an elaborate gravestone in close proximity to the church. Roman examined the engraving.

"This is your great-grandfather, Mikhailo Treshnevsky. He was born in 1864 and died in 1924."

I quickly did the math—he died at age sixty and his timeline fit with Alexander's and Maria's.

We went farther up the hill to the church, but the doors were locked. Volodymyr saw a residence a few yards down from the church that seemed to be part of the church's property.

An elderly woman with a weathered face answered our knock. She and Volodymyr quickly became involved in a lengthy conversation while Roman stood nearby. After about forty-five minutes, she went inside her home, returning with a large key and we proceeded with our climb to the church. The interior of the church held a magnificent collection of gold religious icons and biblical scenes painted in vibrant pastel colors on each wall and the domed ceilings. We kneeled in front of the altar and made an offering. When we exited, Volodymyr continued his conversation with the old woman and then wrote something in his notepad.

Back in the car, Volodymyr told us this story:

"The old woman is the caretaker of the church and remembers the tragic love story of Alexander and Maria very well—it has been handed down through the generations in Krasne.

"When Maria told Alexander she was pregnant, he was happy, and wanted to marry her. They went to Mikhailo to get his permission and blessing, but Mikhailo became angry, stating he would not allow his son to marry a servant girl. He wanted his eldest son to follow in his footsteps and become a priest. When Maria heard his words, 'I will not allow …' she calmly walked out of the rectory, packed her belongings, and moved back to Husne. Alexander did not follow her.

"Krasne residents soon heard about Maria's pregnancy and it became the scandal of the village—but contempt was toward Mikhailo, not Maria. Krasne villagers had become very fond of her. Mikhailo's refusal to allow the marriage angered them. Mikhailo died of a heart attack a few years later, but by then Maria had started a new life in Husne."

As I sat in the backseat of Volodymyr's car listening to this story, I wondered if Mikhailo knew that Maria was pregnant and if it would have made a difference. What did Mikhailo say to Alexander when Maria left? Did he threaten to disinherit him? Even so, the larger fault is on Alexander for not doing the right thing. Perhaps Alexander didn't have the courage to defy his father, knowing he would face a bleak future if disinherited. Or maybe he loved the idea of becoming a priest and a prominent member of society more than he loved Maria. I speculated the latter was true; if Alexander truly loved Maria, nothing would have stopped him from being with her, especially since she was carrying his child.

I thought about Grandmother Maria's marriage to Mihas, which occurred within a year after my mother's birth.

"Did Mihas know Alexander was my mother's father?" I asked Volodymyr.

"No one in Husne knew who had fathered Julia. Many villagers speculated, and a rumor spread: a soldier had raped her. Maria kept the secret of Alexander until she was near the end of her life."

"What was Mihas like?" I asked.

"Mihas descended from a noble clan that owned two-thirds of Ukraine, so he owned a lot of property. The only other benefit of descending from a noble clan was a front row pew in Holy Trinity Greek Catholic Church."

Mother had given this information to me, but at the time I was skeptical. She often told me the story of her classmates addressing her as Pani (Lady) Czeczerska, and that she didn't like it, and had asked her mother to inform the school administration to address her as merely "Julia."

Volodymyr continued, "They didn't live in luxury, like aristocrats. When we get to Husne you'll see for yourself. The original house had a dirt floor, straw roof, and no plumbing, but at least they had a water well, none of the other houses did. There were only three rooms in the house: a kitchen and two bedrooms—one for Maria and Mihas, and their nine children slept in the other bedroom."

Czeczerski Coat of Arms

"Mihas and Maria had nine children?" I asked, bewildered. I had known about Wasyl since the time I was a child, and had learned about Kazia, Polusia, and Anna only a few years ago when I began my search for Wasyl, but the news of nine children completely surprised me.

"Only five survived, the other four, two sets of twins, died in infancy of pneumonia," Volodymyr responded.

"My mother always told me her grandfather, Ivan, mistreated her, and Wasyl stood up to him, telling him he had to treat her better."

"Ivan didn't want Mihas to marry Maria, because of Julia, but he married her anyway."

I thought about Maria's marriage to Mihas. Her marriage to Mihas was soon after Alexander's rejection. Did she love him? Did she marry him because he could give her a good life, the same reason my mother had married Paul? She had never stopped loving Jozef; he had been the love of her life. Did Maria feel the same way about Alexander? Mihas must have loved Maria, because he married her despite his father's opposition. Perhaps Maria loved Mihas because of that.

We arrived in Husne much later than planned due to our unexpected detour to Krasne. Mother's childhood home was exactly where she described it would be, on the right side of the only road going into Husne, next to the church, across the stream leading to the church. I smiled, envisioning Mother and Wasyl catching fish with their bare hands in the stream down the hill from their house.

My Czeczerski relatives had prepared a huge feast for us and then gave us a tour of the homestead: the cow barn, horse stable, vegetable garden, and the snake-infested cellar next to their house where my mother had hidden from Russian and German soldiers. It had been rebuilt and now had a concrete floor, electricity, and was snake-free.

I saw Mount Pikui in the distance—its beauty just as my mother had said it would be.

Dusk descended on Husne by the time we left. Volodymyr and Roman dropped us off in front of our hotel, letting us know what time they'd pick us up the following morning.

About nine that night, the phone rang. Roman excitedly told us that his father had spoken to the wife of the current arch-priest of St. Makovei's Church in Krasne, and she wanted to meet with us, to give us some photographs.

"Of Maria and Alexander?" I anxiously asked.

"Yes."

The next day Volodymyr and Roman drove us a few miles from our hotel to an area of Lviv that seemed to be the business district. We met the arch-priest's wife by a large bronze statue of a Ukrainian hero. After greetings, we walked to a small coffee shop. The woman was holding a large manila envelope and what appeared to be a record book. She and Volodymyr poured through the book immersed in a conversation while I kept eyeing the envelope, anxious to see its contents. When they finally finished their discussion, the woman pulled out several photographs, handing them to Volodymyr. He looked at them, smiling, then handed one to me, saying, "This is a picture of Maria that Alexander kept hidden in his bible his entire life."

I gazed at the picture—a young, happy Maria, posing on the hill in front of the church in Krasne—a photograph of my grandmother that Alexander had carefully placed in his bible for safekeeping. It had been kept and lovingly preserved for nearly one hundred years.

The woman then brought out pictures of Mikhailo and Roman Pasechinsky, explaining who they were, but said she did not have any further information. I thanked her sincerely, content and grateful for being able to solve what I believed at one time to be unsolvable.

When I returned from Ukraine, I immediately went to see Mother. I had been gone for three weeks and she beamed as soon as I entered

My grandmother, Maria Czeczerski, Krasne, Ukraine, 1915.

Roman Pasechinsky, possibly my mother's great-grandfather. Roman was a priest in St. Makovei Ukrainian Orthodox Church, Krasne, Ukraine. Circa pre-1899.

Mikhaylo Treshnevsky, possibly my mother's grandfather.

Left to right seated: Apoloniya Chaykovska Treshnevsky, Mikhaylo Treshnevsky, Alexander Treshnevsky (seated on far right); woman to left of Alexander may be his wife. The two men standing in back are Alexander's two younger brothers. Photo taken at St. Makovei Greek Catholic Church, Krasne, Ukraine, sometime between 1918 and 1924.

the door. I knelt down beside her chair, saying I had very important news.

She looked at me intently.

Mom was ninety-one, and sometimes had difficulty focusing and understanding what was being said. I prayed today would not be one of those days. I wanted her to know and remember what I was about to say.

"Mom, I found out who your father is."

She stared at me, motionless, not breathing.

"He was the son of a priest in Krasne, who was studying to become a priest himself."

She looked at me, confused, still not taking a breath, but I knew she was cognitive. Suddenly she started sobbing.

When she regained her composure, she stammered between sobs that she had lived her entire life thinking her father had been a criminal, someone who had raped her mother, a vile, evil person.

She struggled in her wheelchair, reaching to embrace me. The arthritis made the slightest movement painful; I came as close as I could and she grabbed my hand, kissing it. My mother finally knew who her father was.

FOURTEEN

Legacies

When I began my search for Jozef, I had envisioned uncovering a hero's history, a legacy worthy of my children. Instead, I discovered dishonesty, brutality, and rage; characteristics I never expected in my father, never wanted for their grandfather. I had hoped his life would be a shining example, a past I would be proud to bequeath to his descendants. It wasn't what I imagined, but I've come to terms with the man he really was, and see that every person's story has a valuable lesson; Jozef's was no different. I finally understood that the sum of who my father was didn't define me. I had to look inside myself for that. My own words and deeds define me.

My children are grown now and have an appreciation of their ancestors, their European history, and the extraordinary event of WWII that led them to becoming Americans. Even though Jozef was not distinguished with honors, nor were any of my other family members, they gave me their unique stories, sometimes laudable, sometimes painfully tragic. I consider myself fortunate, proud to share them with my children and grandchildren.

I now have twenty-seven gold-embossed leather photo albums full of pictures of my Sutton, Kurek, and Czeczerski family members. If ever there is a fire in my house and I can only save a few valuables, it would be those albums that would be rescued. During that blizzard in Denver, while I carefully placed each photo of Keith's family in our albums, I came to the realization that the pictures and stories were all that remained for us to remember our families. I know my worldly possessions will be discarded, donated to Goodwill, sold, or distributed among my children. But the albums, with Great-grandfather Emery's Certificate of Honorable Discharge from the Union Army, and the portrait of Grandmother Maria, happy and smiling on the hill of St. Makovei's Church in Krasne, will become part of our family story relived by future generations. My grandson, Keith Paul Sutton, will inherit the albums that now include pictures of a long-lost family from a faraway place and time. I hope the story that gets passed down to my descendants is that Grandmother Sutton searched for her lost family for forty-three years—and found them—and that's how these photo albums came to be.

Jozef, Mom, Wasyl, and Dad had been swept into World War II and it changed their destinies, the same as the war had changed the course of history. When my son Bradley first read about Hitler, Stalin, and WWII, he thought it fascinating, profoundly moving. That he didn't know the full extent of the atrocities of war—the *stalags*, executions, forced labor, rapes, torture, and DP camps—disquieted me. As George

Left: Kazia Czeczerska, Nizne Husne, Ukraine, 1946.
Right: Anna and Polusia Czeczerska, Nizne Husne, Ukraine, 1946.

Anna Czeczerska, Nizne Husne, Ukraine, 2006.

Above left: Polusia Czeczerska, Stryj, Ukraine, 2007.
Above: Wasyl and Kazia Hromyk, Nizne Husne, Ukraine, circa early 1960s.
Left: Left to right: Anna, Maria, Kazia, and Wasyl Hromyk (names of children unknown), Nizne Husne, Ukraine, circa late 1940s or early '50s.

Left to right seated: Kazia Czeczerska Hromyk; Katerynia and Oksana Hromyk (Volodymyr's daughter and wife). Standing left to right: Roman Khorkavyi (Katerynia's father), and Volodymyr Hromyk (Kazia's son), Lviv, Ukraine, 1991.

Santayana, the renowned Spanish philosopher said, "Those who cannot remember the past are condemned to repeat it."

I cannot fathom the atrocities committed during WWII, and it is difficult for me to understand how Hitler could persuade ordinary German citizens to commit heinous crimes against humanity. During the Nuremberg trials, Hermann Goering, one of the Nazi party's top leaders, explained it this way:

> "Voice or no voice, the people can always be brought to the bidding of their leaders. That is easy. All you have to do is tell them they are being attacked and denounce the pacificists for lack of patriotism and exposing the country to danger. It works the same way in any country."

When I remember my mother studying for her citizenship exam, recalling the words that gave me a deep love and respect for America,

"We the people," and "Inalienable rights," I think about our war on terror and Benjamin Franklin's famous statement when he addressed the Pennsylvania Assembly in 1755: "They who would give up an essential liberty for temporary security deserve neither liberty nor security."

History is the teacher of the future, and pictures help us remember. When General Dwight Eisenhower, the Supreme Commander of the Allied Forces entered the death camps, he ordered photographs be taken, to be used as evidence of war crimes, and so that future generations could see the atrocities. After I found Wasyl, I learned I have many cousins, scattered throughout the world. General Eisenhower chose my cousin Walter Chichersky (the Americanized spelling of Czeczerski), to be one of the photographers who immortalized those historic images. At age seventeen, Walter enlisted in the Army Signal Corps at the outbreak of World War II, serving as a combat soldier and then as a photographer for General George S. Patton. He was one of only a few soldiers to hold a pass from General Dwight D. Eisenhower allowing him admittance to any restricted area for taking photos. Walter was the first photographer to enter Buchenwald concentration camp in Germany. Some of his work is displayed in the National Archives and in the United States Holocaust Memorial Museum. His historic photographs were used as primary evidence to help convict high-ranking Nazis at the war trials at the conclusion of WWII held at Nuremberg, Germany.

When I began my journey to find my father, I wanted my children to know of the heroism and bravery of my ancestors, and that they, too, had fought hard and died for freedom. I have found those stories, and although Jozef's life was not what I had imagined or wanted it to be, I learned valuable, life-changing lessons can be discovered from every person's life.

I look at the pictures of my family quite often. When I look at the pictures of Kazia, Polusia, and Anna, I see three young girls screaming in horror at the sight of their brother Wasyl being shoved toward the door by soldiers pointing guns at him. They were too young to be taken into forced labor and lived in Ukraine their entire lives without stepping outside its borders.

Kazia and her children inherited the large acreage of Czeczerski land in Husne that would have belonged to Wasyl, but he has no interest to claim it, stating his life and home are in America. Husne is still a primitive village and Kazia's children work hard bailing hay and loading it on horse-drawn wagons. Her son Volodymyr became a journalist, one of the few in Ukraine granted a visa to tour America with other reporters. He owns a successful publishing company.

Polusia became a servant to a family living in Stryj, but their house, a three room frame, is not a mansion and the family would be considered impoverished by American standards. She lives in a small shack a few feet from the main house. At age four, she broke her back and is hunched, unable to stand straight.

Anna lived in Husne her entire life. Her son Nicholai and his wife Marika have four sons and a daughter. I get telephone calls in the middle of the night from Marika. She doesn't speak English, but can understand it. Her neighbor speaks English and helps translate. We usually have a disjointed conversation in our brief telephone calls.

When I look at my grandmother Maria's picture, I see a vibrant, beautiful young woman falling in love with a priest's son, being betrayed by him, yet keeping his secret. I see her as a woman who calmed her daughter's fears by giving her a fragile picture of the Virgin Mary to comfort and protect her while she hid in dark, frigid cellars and thick underbrush, waiting for soldiers to leave. I wonder what agonies Maria suffered witnessing Julia and Wasyl, her two eldest children, being hauled away by German soldiers.

I can visualize Maria, determined, desperate, and courageous, sitting in a cold, dank room, writing a letter to Hitler by candlelight, begging and demanding her children's release. It saddens me to think that Maria died in 1970 without knowing what happened to her daughter, without ever meeting her grandchildren and great-grandchildren.

When I look at the picture of Wasyl, I see a young boy standing up to his grandfather, demanding he treat Julia better; a young man fighting for Ukraine's independence only to have it lost again to Stalin after WWII; and I see the brother risking his own life and freedom to bring Julia food and water while she is hiding in mountains and cold, snake-infested cellars, waiting for soldiers to leave.

When I look at photos of Dad, I see a knight in shining armor who made the dream of America possible for an abandoned family. His marriage to my mother was nothing short of a miracle. At age forty-seven, my stepfather began a new life, having lost his homeland, property, and family during WWII. He made the best of it, never complaining about his loss. Dad worked hard to give Mom, Krys, and me a good life, never expecting anything in return. Although Mom could not reciprocate Dad's love for her, she gave him the best care, and made him happy. My one regret is that Dad went to his deathbed without ever knowing how much I truly loved him.

When I look at Jozef's picture now, I see the man I had been searching for forty-three years, and the discrepancy between my image of him and the reality. After his marriage to Helene in 1958, Jozef never wrote to his sister Stanislawa. She died in 1980 not knowing what happened to him. Her son found Jozef's letters and photos in a box in the attic, but threw them away. When I asked Helene and Angelica if they had some small, inexpensive item of Jozef's such as a pen or a comb, they said that after his death they had gotten rid of his belongings. It wasn't until I returned from my visit with Angelica that Mother told me about the old washtub Jozef had stolen from a German farmer—the one that had carried our worldly possessions to America. It's the only item he touched that I have. The washtub is stored in the corner of my basement, cracked and rusted. Sometimes I touch it, just to momentarily connect with Jozef. People may wonder why I would want to be close to Jozef, and my only explanation is that, without him, I would not be here.

I often wonder if Jozef would have been a different person if Germany had not invaded Poland and he was able to realize his dreams.

Mom, Dad, and Wasyl had their dreams shattered, too, but managed to overcome their obstacles and rebuild their lives. If my children are ever faced with that kind of adversity, I hope their kindness and goodness will prevail. Thomas Paine said: "If there must be trouble, let it be in my day, that my child may have peace."

If I could say anything to Jozef today, it would be, "Why did you choose cruelty and anger instead of kindness and love?"

When I look at my mother, I see traces of the young woman who loved to dance, like her mother, Maria. I see a young girl waiting for her life to begin on her front porch in Husne on a warm summer night, and a woman chopping wood in the bitter cold, brutalized by the farmer's young daughter, and beaten. I see her falling in love with the handsome Polish officer with sun-colored hair and piercing blue eyes, giving birth to his daughters, and then being abandoned. I see a woman avoiding the uncertainty of post-war Poland, marrying a man she did not love, and learning to love him in her own way.

I am struck by the many ironies in this journey of the heart. Throughout my life I have been looking at the stars in the night sky, wondering where Jozef and Wasyl were. It is poetic that Wasyl was living in a city named after Bethlehem, where the brightest star shined.

Another irony is that Krystyna and her family lived in New Jersey for more than twenty years—just seventy-five miles from where Wasyl and Anna were. Over the course of two decades, Krys and her husband Bob have gone to the Bethlehem historic district during Christmastime. Anna and Wasyl also visited at the same time of year. They could have passed each other and never known it.

Anna and Wasyl vacationed in many of the same places as Krys and Bob: Atlantic City, Orlando, Niagara Falls, and Myrtle Beach. What if they had bumped into each other, started a conversation and introduced themselves? Surely, as soon as Wasyl said the name "Czeczerski," Krys would have told him her mother's maiden name and the mystery would have been solved twenty years sooner. We could have had two decades of family memories, holidays, birthdays, and the other events life brings. But I try not to think of what could have been.

A third irony is that I live less than five hundred miles from Renatta, the daughter of Jozef and Helene's next door neighbors in Dachau. Angelica often stayed with Renatta during Jozef's alcoholic rages. The world can be so large and small at the same time.

The discovery of Jozef being my biological father while listening to Ricky Nelson singing *Travelin' Man*, albeit trite, is nonetheless an irony because I have traveled the world over searching for my lost family.

Wasyl and Helene have said, "I've been here for over fifty years, and I've had nothing to hide—why didn't you find me sooner?"

In my heart, I know I did everything possible. I spent thousands of hours sending emails and letters, visiting foreign countries, and paying huge sums to strangers to find them. What I've learned from my journey is that no matter how much love or money you have, your success depends on the goodness of others and an intangible, indefinable force. I wish I had been able to find Jozef before he died and Wasyl while he and Mother were younger and still had good health. I console myself with the simple explanation, "It wasn't meant to be."

Most people hearing my story ask me what my feelings were at the exact moment of finding my father, uncle, and maternal grandfather. I found Jozef and learned of his death at the same time, in the same email. His death disappointed, but did not surprise me. Mother had prepared me emotionally. The likelihood of finding him alive had diminished with each passing year. I felt relief more than anything else; my lifelong search was over. The emotional trauma came when I finally realized, then accepted, who Jozef really was.

The experience of finding my uncle Wasyl was quite different. I had a moment of pure silence and peace in my heart, and then the enormity of the event overwhelmed me.

As to finding Alexander, I never expected to solve the mystery of who my mother's father was. The discovery of Alexander is an amazing gift that was just handed to me. During our last day in Ukraine, Volodymyr asked me what my favorite place was. I thought of the beautiful places Keith and I had visited: the Crimea, Yalta, Swallows Nest, the Cossack fortress, and the gold domes of Kiev, but my response to him was a sincere "Krasne." Someday I will try to find Alexander's family, hoping that they, too, have had a good life and will be happy to meet me.

Some people ask me if I worried about my stepfather's feelings during my lifelong search for Jozef. I never told Dad about my infatuation with Jozef. I didn't think I could adequately explain to him that my need to find my biological father had nothing to do with my feelings for him. Paul had been a good father. Paul Venckus was the only grandfather my children had ever known. Sadly, he died at the age of ninety-one, without ever knowing how much I loved and admired him. I never heard my mom tell him, "I love you," and I didn't think it would be appropriate for me to say those words to him. He died before I became wise enough to know I should have told him.

Another question I get asked is, "Was it worth all the time, money, and heartbreak to find your family?" I don't have to think about the answer—it is an unequivocal and resounding "Yes!" I didn't have a history or sense of belonging before I found my family. Finding them has made me whole, no longer disconnected.

Some people find it incredulous that I would search for my family for forty-three years, and at times I, too, find it hard to believe. I became discouraged quite often, to the point of giving up, but I drew my inspiration to continue the search from an email message I received in the wee small hours of the night, from a stranger in a distant place also searching for her lost family. Her message simply said, "Seek and Ye Shall Find" (Luke 11:5–8; Mathew 7:7).

I wish I could tell Jozef what a wonderful family he had. To think of all Jozef missed. He could have witnessed Mother's brilliant smile at the birth of her grandchildren Cindie and Brad. I wonder if he ever realized what a remarkable person she was. Through all the heartbreak he caused, she still loved him and would have been overjoyed to have him by her side watching their grandchildren grow. But it was Paul who was there for them, who taught them things—gardening, dominoes, and about life in the Old Country. He'd talk to Brad about the war and our coming to America. Whenever he spoke, Dad combined the English, German, Polish, and Lithuanian languages, but Brad could understand everything he said. Brad named his own son after Grandpa Paul because he admired him so much.

My daughter Cindie has been inspired by Maria Czeczerski's courage and her valiant efforts to rescue her children, by daring to write Hitler. Each time Cindie is challenged in her personal or professional life, she told me, she finds strength in Maria's bravery.

Both Cindie and Brad are American citizens by birth, reaping the hard-won benefits of what my mother endured. Cindie is a successful real estate agent; like Jozef, everyone she meets likes her instantly. Besides her blonde hair and blue eyes, she also inherited Jozef's charisma. People notice her. She is a thoughtful and caring person, incapable of Jozef's cruelty.

My son Brad inherited Jozef's height: At six-foot-two, his presence is impressive in a crowd. I see Jozef when Brad becomes restless, and I look for other signs of his grandfather in his behavior, but I only see a considerate and kind man, much more like my husband.

A real estate appraiser, Brad is the founder and CEO of his own small corporation, and works long hours to make his business succeed.

I still ponder what Jozef's reaction would be to everything.

My mother frequently says, "I didn't give you up! Everyone said I was stupid to keep you and Krys, but I listened to my heart and my mother's voice in my dream saying, 'If God gives you children, he will help you raise them.' I brought you to America with me so we could all have a better life." Even now, when I visit Mom at Assisted Living, in her private room decorated with her antiques, pictures of family, the conversation may turn to Germany and Mom still has the need to tell me, "I didn't give you up."

She doesn't have to reassure me. I know that keeping Krys and me was the best and most important decision Mom ever made. She has no regrets. She married Paul to keep us together, to bring us to America. She married Paul even though her heart belonged to Jozef. Not once in my life, no matter how angry or hurt I was, did I ever say or think I wished my mother had given me up. Her fervent love for Krys and me was apparent, and unconditional.

Today, my mother is no longer the vibrant, exuberant person Wasyl remembers; Krystyna reminds him of Mom when she was young. Mom can no longer do much other than sit in her recliner or sleep in her bed, her memory fading. When I returned from my trip to Ukraine in 2009, and visited Mom in her room at Raleigh Gardens Assisted Living Center to inform her Alexander Treshnevsky was her father, stating that all the family mysteries had been solved, I thought of the yellowed documents in the aqua blue metal box and the discrepancies in her date of birth. I finally felt free to ask her. She answered, "Everyone in the DP camps wanted to immigrate to America, and we heard young people had a better chance, so I changed my birthday—it made the difference of being in my twenties instead of thirties." I smiled. I had speculated on a number of reasons for the change, but had overlooked the most logical explanation.

In part, my purpose for writing this book is that her memories, her story, and that of my father Paul, Uncle Wasyl, and Jozef will endure. I wanted it for my children and grandchildren. I wanted other people to know their courage, strength, resiliency, and their weaknesses and faults; after all, they were human.

A number of my friends, acquaintances, and colleagues who, upon hearing this extraordinary story, say, "I didn't know you were Jewish!" I am amazed they didn't know Catholic families in Eastern Europe were executed, too. World War II was a tragedy of enormous proportions—almost 43 million people died. Six million were Jewish, and seven million were Slavic. WWII was a holocaust for mankind.

When I look back, I wonder how the lives of Jozef, Wasyl, and my mother would have turned out if Germany had not invaded Poland. Would Jozef have lived the adventurous life he had wanted? Would Wasyl have become an important elected official?

Wasyl had two remaining wishes: to touch the soil of Ukraine again, and to place a headstone on his father Mihas' unmarked grave. When I visited Ukraine, I arranged to bring back a small bag of sterilized soil, placing it in a small, elaborately hand-carved wooden box, with "Ukraine" inscribed in Cyrillic on its lid. When Wasyl opened it, he touched the soil and cried, saying, "I fought for you to be free."

I could not give Wasyl his final wish; his father is buried among five other unmarked graves—but he accepts that Mihas will be one of the thousands of victims whose final resting place will remain unknown.

Mother's life may have turned out quite differently. Perhaps she would have become a nurse in Ukraine and married the schoolteacher who had shown an interest in her. Would she have claimed the property Oluzia had bequeathed to her and lived in Husne her entire life, or would she have become a servant, as did Polusia?

I wonder if Jozef turned to alcohol because the abandonment of my mother and his infant daughters cut to his conscience, or did he even care? Did he become an alcoholic during the endless days in the DP camps? Something in Jozef's life made him turn to alcohol for comfort. I will never know what it was.

I do know that what seemed to be the worst events in my mother's life became the turning points for the best and led her to her final destiny, a good life in America.

I have come away from this sojourn with a tranquil heart. At age ninety-one, Mom learned who her father was. She had never spoken of the anguish of not knowing, but when I told her she sobbed with relief, admitting for the first time in her life that she had been afraid of whom he might be.

My one remaining mystery to solve is to find Alexander Treshnevsky's descendants. Scraps of information helped me solve the mystery of Jozef, and I'm depending on the sheets of paper I am now collecting in a tabulated binder to help me find Alexander. I hope his family will be happy to learn he was my grandfather.

Mom and Wasyl can leave this good earth in peace knowing what happened to each other. I gave my children and grandchildren the gift of family and history—family being the greatest gift of all.

Mom, Dad, and Uncle Wasyl came here with, as they say, "only the shirts on their backs," fulfilling their dream of America. They learned English, secured good jobs, worked hard, and saved money to buy their own homes. They endured some of the greatest adversities in their lives, yet they were happy, caring, loving people—that is their true legacy to my children, grandchildren, and me.

The Czeczerski family turned out to be everything I had hoped they would be—kind, loving, friendly, with an unquenchable zest for life and a deep respect for their country. I learned that I have a large extended Czeczerski family living in Pennsylvania, Florida, Canada, and Ukraine.

The Kureks have also been kind and loving, unconditionally accepting me into their family. They, too, are friendly, outgoing, happy people with a strong allegiance to their country.

Mother talks to Wasyl several times every day, mostly about their childhood in Husne—digging hazelnuts, fishing with their hands, and eating vine-ripened berries from the lush Carpathian hills.

A question that comes to mind is, "What is the point in having relatives on the other side of the world, unable to readily communicate due to the language barrier?" The answer is simple—If they ever need me, I will be there for them. That is the purpose of family.

I have visited my mother's birthplace, climbed the green hills of the Carpathian Mountains, and feasted on the berries growing wild on its slopes and valleys. I have seen the magnificent gold domes of Ukraine's majestic buildings, constructed on top of green hills, some of which are covered with thousands of white crosses marking the graves of Stalin's victims.

Sometimes the gold domes are obscured by black smoke billowing from the few remaining Communist-era factories. The USSR had built many munitions factories and warehouse-looking apartments in Ukraine; most are now abandoned and dilapidated, their austere block-style Stalinistic architecture a harsh contrast to the lush landscape and opulent architecture of Ukraine's glorious past. I feel that faraway land is also my home.

I have found what was missing in my life and it has made me happy and whole; although not in the way I thought it would, but it has made me stronger. Jozef did not turn out to be the hero I had wanted him to be. When I started my search for him, I thought everything I was, was because of him. I blamed my mother for Jozef's abandonment, thinking she had not lived up to his expectations. It never occurred to me that my mother would become the hero of this story. In the end, Mom *is* the hero of this story because in spite of all she has lost, she is not bitter. For all the tragedies she has had to endure, she has continued to be loving and caring. She still has a contagious laugh. That special ethereal quality about her that saved her life is a zest for living, boundless love, and a genuine concern for people.

Many people have asked me, "What is the meaning, or purpose, to finding your family?" It is no less an important question than, "What is the meaning of life?" Both questions can only be answered by the person asking the question. We need to believe we have a purpose in life, and we also need to feel we are part of a family. Only we can provide the answer to the purpose of our existence and our need for family.

Those are the stories of my family. I hope you have—or will—find your own family story, because that is what you will be remembered by.

And, I can look at the brilliant stars of the night sky once again and feel the same contentment as when I was a child of four, sitting with my mother and sister on the stoop of our first home in America, and being grateful to be here.

Resources

Andrew Bellenkes—Rank information

Anthony Schlega, Photo Credits, Cossack Chapel, Luttensee Mountain

Artur Mokrzycki

Bank Nederlandse Gemeenten

Bank of the Dutch Municipalities

Barbara DeSantis

Bavaria—Wikipedia; en.wikipedia.org

Bolekchrobry.tripod.com/polishinformationcenter

Carol Burton

Catholic Encyclopedia: Poland

CNN Cold War—Historical Document; Potsdam Agreement; www.cnn.com

Dachau; library.thinkquest.org

Displaced Person Transports: Cargo of Hope; Displaced Person Transportation, post-World War II; www.usmm.org

DP Camps in Europe; www.dpcamps.org

Electronic Museum, Katyn Memorial Wall; www.electronicmuseum.ca

Freytag&berndt road map: Deutschland

Freytag&berndt road map: Poland

Genealogy and Poland on the Internet and elsewhere; www.polishroots.org

GI—World War II Commemoration; gi.Grolier.com

Halyna Myroniuk

History of the Dachau Concentration Camp; members.aol.com

History.acusd.edu—WWII Timeline 1939

Innovative Twinning of Cities; www.usm.my

International Civic Heraldry—Deutsche Kreiswappen-Schongau; www.ngw.nl

John Woodward
Katyn Forest Massacre; Polish deaths at Soviet hands; www.geocities.com
List of German Municipalities; www.faerber.much.de
Louis FitzGibbon: Katyn Massacre, "The Lost 10,000" www.vho.org
Manfred Hellmann, Daten der Polnischen Geschichte, Munchen, 1985
Mario Paesani—Flag icons
Mark Wyman, DPs: Europe's Displaced Persons, 1945–1951
Mary Niesluchowska
Nazi Blitzkrieg; Poland, 1939; www.polandsholocaust.org
Olga Kaczmar; okaczmar@earthlink.net
Piotr Kurek
Poland in the classroom: http://wings.buffalo.edu
Polska; Poland in Brief; www.msz.gov.pl
Professor Zdzislaw P. Wesolowski, Captain, U.S. Air Force Reserve, Restired; Polish Military History Books
Renaissance Warfare by S.A. Jasinski; http://polisharmies
Rodziny; The Journal of the Polish Genealogical Society of America
Russia; www.ostviking.homestead.com
Schongau County; www.fotw.net
Second World War (1939–1945) Military History Wars; www.rickard.karoo.nsf
Siberia; History; www.infoplease.com
Siberia; www.english.upenn.edu
Slave Labor in Concentration Camps; www.dpcamps.org
Stalag XIV; www.pegasus-one.org
The History Place—World War Two in Europe Timeline; wysiwyg; www.historyplace.com
The Sarmation Review; sarmatia@ruf.rice.edu
The Treaty of Versailles; http://www.historylearningsite.co.uk
Thomas Hollowak
World History at KMLA, History of Poland
World War II Lecture Notes; wysiwyg
World War Two Timeline—Poland 1939; www.polandsholocaust.org